The Cathedral Basilica of Saint Louis

An Illustrated Timeline

by John C. Guenther, FAIA, LEED AP

Dedication

This book is dedicated to all those who helped to make the Cathedral Basilica of Saint Louis a reality, each in their own way, all forming a magnificent mosaic of history—of this great cathedral, the City of St. Louis, and our region.

Reedy Press
PO Box 5131
St. Louis, MO 63139, USA
reedypress.com

Library of Congress Control Number: 2025936735

ISBN: 9781681066028

Design by Rich Roden

Unless otherwise noted, all photos are courtesy of the author or believed to be in the public domain.

Cover photos: Front: Photograph by Sam Fentress ©SAM FENTRESS PHOTOGRAPHY. Back: *(third from left)* Courtesy of Archdiocese of St. Louis Archives, *(far right)* Courtesy of Cathedral Basilica of Saint Louis Archives.

Printed in Canada
25 26 27 28 29 5 4 3 2 1

Table of Contents

Introduction

When one thinks of the great cathedrals of the world, thoughts turn to magnificent structures of grand and majestic scale, vast proportions, both exterior and interior, reaching toward the heavens, in contemplation of the glory of God and creation. Stained glass windows and mosaics communicate spiritual lessons and biblical stories. An elaborate altar under a baldacchino creates the focal point of worship. Interiors resonate with music emanating from the towering organ pipes. Dramatic ceilings inspire and speak of majesty. Articulated and finely crafted stone walls create dignified expressions of grandeur.

One also thinks of the span of time, dedicated efforts, and lifelong commitments of so many to realize these great cathedrals—from the spiritual leaders to the faithful flock to the craftspeople and artists who built these magnificent places of worship to those who continue to maintain and enhance them.

These great cathedrals also mark the passage of time and important historical events of the cities and countries in which they are located, as members of their communities gather to worship, celebrate, and mourn.

The Cathedral Basilica of Saint Louis rightfully takes its place among the great cathedrals of the world.

The design of the Cathedral Basilica of Saint Louis grew out of an international competition with a detailed code of requirements. The St. Louis firm of Barnett, Haynes & Barnett emerged as the selected architectural firm from a group of firms best known for ecclesiastical design from Austria, France, Germany, and the United States.

The Romanesque Revival exterior and Byzantine Revival interior design of the Cathedral Basilica of Saint Louis create one of the most significant ecclesiastical buildings in the Western Hemisphere. The cathedral features the Western world's largest collection of mosaics, covering 83,000 square feet of the cathedral's interior, composed of more than 41.5 million pieces of glass tesserae in 7,000 shades of color. The mosaics depict biblical scenes from the Old and New Testaments as well as the principal doctrines of the Catholic Church and its history in the United States, with an emphasis on the St. Louis area. The Byzantine-style mosaics were designed and created by multiple artists and craftspeople over a period of 76 years. The cathedral mosaics are larger than those of St. Mark's Basilica in Venice, Italy.

Whether you are one of the millions who have visited the Cathedral Basilica of Saint Louis or are planning your first visit to this magnificent place of inspiration, art, architecture, history, and spirituality, it is my hope that the beauty and uniqueness of this book as an illustrated timeline will allow the reader to study the various moments that make up the rich story of the Cathedral Basilica of Saint Louis and its inextricable connections with the history of St. Louis and this region, allowing for a deeper appreciation and new insights, as we connect the dots of history.

I was truly moved by the words of Msgr. James T. Telthorst (1942–2022), rector (1991–2002), when he addressed the cathedral parishioners in the August 2000 *St. Louis Cathedral Parish Guide Book and Directory*: "Perhaps a mosaic, in the end, is our best comparison, as each of us adds to the beauty of the parish family and creates a magnificent design for the glory of God."

Indeed, when one reflects on the history of the Cathedral Basilica of Saint Louis and all those who dedicated their lives and efforts to its realization, perhaps "a mosaic . . . is our best comparison" as each of them contributed their part to the beauty we behold today.

—John C. Guenther, FAIA, LEED AP, architect
President, Society of Architectural Historians–St. Louis Chapter

The choir loft, beatitudes, and east/west galleries at the Cathedral Basilica of Saint Louis

Photograph by Sam Fentress, © SAM FENTRESS PHOTOGRAPHY

Acknowledgments

To write this book that illuminates key moments over 352 years of history and traces the development and growth of the United States and the Midwest region, the establishment of the City of St. Louis, the influence of Catholicism, and the building of the Basilica of St. Louis, King of France (Old Cathedral) (1834); St. John the Apostle and Evangelist Church (1860)–the Pro-Cathedral (1864–1914); and the Cathedral Basilica of Saint Louis (1914–present), with its design, development, construction, installation, and completion of its magnificent mosaics, and key moments in time with illustrations, was a monumental task made possible by the generous help of many who allowed me access to their archival materials and shared their vast knowledge and deep insights.

I want to express my deep gratitude and thanks to the following individuals and organizations for their invaluable help and assistance:

Msgr. Henry Breier, rector, for granting me access to the Cathedral Basilica of Saint Louis Archives, with their artifacts, articles, and records of the design and completion of the Cathedral Basilica of Saint Louis. I thank Mary Ann Fox, events manager, who accompanied me during my photography of the interiors of the Cathedral Basilica of Saint Louis. Eric Fair, CA, director of archives and records, and Rena Schergen, MSLIS, CA, archivist, both of Archdiocese of St. Louis, for all of their help and support in granting me access to review and study the archival records and images of the Cathedral Basilica of Saint Louis, which bring the history of the cathedral to life. Thomas R. Du Bois, director of building and real estate, Archdiocese of St. Louis, for sharing information and images of key restoration projects of the Cathedral Basilica of Saint Louis. Dennis Northcott, associate archivist for reference, Archives Department, Missouri Historical Society Library and Research Center, for his guidance and research on the files of the Cathedral Basilica of Saint Louis. Mary C. Eggleston, reference archivist, Jesuit Archives & Research Center, and Katie Mascari, Saint Louis University Archives, for their insights and help with archival images.

Charles E. Brown, Langenberg curator of reference, UMSL university archivist, and John Neal Hoover, endowed Mercantile Library executive director, both of the St. Louis Mercantile Library, University of Missouri–St. Louis, for allowing me access to the St. Louis Globe-Democrat Collection, with its historical photographs and articles documenting important events related to the Cathedral Basilica of Saint Louis. Mary Beth Drabiszczak, assistant archivist, Conrad Schmitt Studios, Inc., of New Berlin, Wisconsin, who provided archival information on the al secco mosaic-paintings of the east and west transept half domes implemented by their firm 1924–25. Trent Sindelar and the St. Louis Public Library–Central Library for the use of *The Notable Catholic Institutions of St. Louis and Vicinity,* Francis A. Thornton, A.M., Theodore Adlemann, George D. Barnett, The Finkenbiner-Reid Publishing Co., 1911, which offered valuable insights and photographs of the construction of the Cathedral Basilica of Saint Louis. Nicholas Frei, Emil Frei & Associates. Nicholas, fifth generation of the Frei family, graciously shared his invaluable insights and research on the history of the Emil Frei Art Glass Company and Ravenna Mosaics, Inc., both founded by Emil Frei, Sr., Nicholas's great-great-grandfather. His research in the Emil Frei & Associates archives and other archival sources has clarified, confirmed, and corrected certain dates regarding the mosaic designs and implementation, along with historical photographs which illustrate key moments in time.

And last, but certainly not least, I want to express my thanks and deep gratitude to my wife, Jane Guenther, M.Div., who is my first editor in all endeavors.

—With deep gratitude,
John C. Guenther, FAIA, LEED AP, Architect

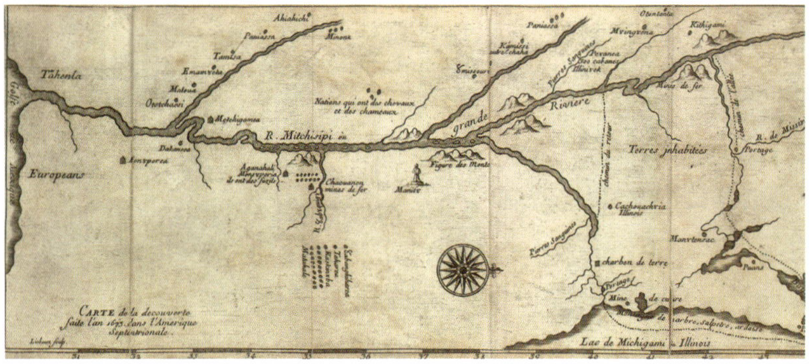

Map of the Jolliet- Marquette 1673 expedition, ca. 1681

Courtesy of Library of Congress, Geography and Map Division, Washington, DC

Wilhelm Lamprecht, German, 1838–1901

Père Marquette and the Indians, 1869

Oil on canvas, 43 1/2 x 53 x 0 in

00.3

Gift of Rev. Stanislaus P. Lalumiere, S.J.

Haggerty Museum of Art, Marquette University

1673: The Jolliet-Marquette Expedition

The Reverend Jacques Marquette was born at Laon, France, on June 1, 1637, and joined the Society of Jesus at age 17 in 1654. After numerous requests to serve as a missionary, the Jesuits assigned him to New France in 1666 to serve the Indigenous peoples of the Americas. Marquette went on to found the St. Ignace mission in 1671 in the Upper Peninsula of Michigan near the Straits of Mackinac.

Louis Jolliet, a young Canadian born on September 21, 1645, in Beaupré, a French settlement near Quebec City, was educated by the Jesuits and considered the priesthood before leaving the seminary to become a fur trader.

Marquette and Jolliet departed from St. Ignace on May 17, 1673, with two canoes and five voyageurs of French and Indigenous American ancestry. They crossed Lake Michigan to Green Bay and traveled up the Fox River. From there, they portaged their canoes a short distance to the Wisconsin River (near today's Portage, Wisconsin), later entering the Mississippi River on June 17, 1673, near present-day Prairie du Chien, Wisconsin.

The word *Mississippi* comes from the Ojibwe (Algonquin language family) word *Messipi* or *Misi-ziibi*, which means "Great River" or "Gathering of Waters."

The Jolliet-Marquette Expedition traveled down the Mississippi River. Along the way, they met friendly Indigenous tribes along the Iowa banks, and they discovered the Illinois River entering from the east; the mighty Missouri River, whose "water was very muddy"; a fantastic bird painted on a sheer cliff on the east side—the Piasa; and the limestone rise above the river to the west that would later become St. Louis. They continued on to the mouth of the Arkansas River, where they turned back north.

The voyageurs followed the Mississippi back to the Illinois River, reaching the confluence on about July 17, 1673, taking the shorter route back to the Great Lakes, as suggested by friendly natives. By the fall of 1673, the explorers were in the Straits of Mackinac, with Jolliet off to report to authorities in Quebec.

1698: Missions in the Illinois Country

Following Jolliet and Marquette's expedition of 1673, René-Robert Cavelier, Sieur de La Salle (1643–87) canoed the lower Mississippi River from the mouth of the Illinois River to the Gulf of Mexico in early 1682. On April 9, he claimed the Mississippi River basin for France, naming it *La Louisiane*, in honor of Saint Louis (Louis IX) and Louis XIV of France. The Louisiana Territory extended from the Appalachians to the Rockies.

In the 1690s, the Jesuits returned to the Indigenous Illini. Father François Pinet was with the Chicago nation, while the Franciscan Recollect Fathers Paul Binneteau and Gabriel Marest worked with the Peorias, the Kaskaskias, the Tamaroas, and other nations.

To the surprise of the Jesuits, three diocesan priests from Quebec, formed at the Seminary of Quebec and known as "the Gentlemen of the Seminary," were trained to work among the Indigenous peoples and were sent by Bishop Saint-Vallier to take charge of the Illinois country.

Fathers François de Montigny, Antoine Davion, and Jean-François Buisson de Saint-Cosme traveled south to carry on their apostolic work. Leaving the Illinois River, they paddled into the Mississippi River on December 3, 1698; saw the Piasa Bird; and arrived at Cahokia on December 7, 1698. On the eighth day of that month, the three seminary priests traveled from Cahokia to the west bank of the river to celebrate the feast of the Immaculate Conception with Mass. The priests took turns celebrating Mass on a large stone set on a limestone rise above the river, near present-day Arsenal Street, on what would be known as the Day of Three Masses. This site would become part of the settlement of Saint Louis 66 years later, when the town was founded by Frenchmen Pierre Laclède and René-Auguste Chouteau in 1764. The year 1698 therefore marks the beginning of the Catholic story of St. Louis.

In 1699, Father Jean Bergier, a Seminary priest from Canada, came to Cahokia to lay the foundations of the new parish named *Sainte Famille*, French for "Holy Family." After erecting a cross, a log chapel, and a log rectory, the first log church was dedicated on May 14, 1699. Bergier was joined by Father Jean-François Buisson de Saint-Cosme in 1700. The second log church was built in 1799, in the French colonial poteaux-sur-sol (post-on-sill) vertical-log construction method, replacing the first church, which burned about 1740. The black-walnut vertical timbers, built from the logs salvaged from the original church, lean inward, strengthening the structure. It was dedicated on September 24, 1799. It is the oldest church west of the Allegheny Mountains. This log church, built in a French Colonial style, is one of only five that still exist in North America.

Guillaume de l'Isle's *Map of Louisiana and the Mississippi River* (1718). From the collections of the St. Louis Mercantile Library, University of Missouri–St. Louis

Holy Family Log Church

Cahokia, Illinois, dedicated May 14, 1699, burned about 1740, rebuilt and dedicated September 24, 1799

Photograph by John C. Guenther, FAIA, LEED AP

1700: The Middle Valley–East Bank

In 1700, the Kaskaskias on the upper Illinois River, along with some of their Christian neighbors, were coming under attack by the Shawnees and others. To achieve peace and security, the Jesuits suggested a migration to the south should be undertaken to seek protection. The great Black Robe of the day, the Jesuit Father Jacques Gravier explored the Mississippi River lower valley for a suitable location. Fathers Pinet and Marest followed with the Kaskaskias and their friends down the Illinois River to the Mississippi River, where they wintered on the west bank near a little river, later known as the *Rivière des Pères*. Their stay lasted from 1700 to 1702 before they traveled further downstream, settling on the east bank. In the spring of 1703, they established the village of Kaskaskia, now in Randolph County, Illinois.

Kaskaskia grew to be an important destination between Cahokia and points further south. The town layout reflected its French origins, with large square blocks divided into four quadrants set in a grid of streets. The Jesuit Fathers Gabriel Marest (1662–1714) and Jean Mermet (1664–1716) and others served Kaskaskia, while the Gentlemen of the Seminary from Quebec served Cahokia.

In 1720, the French government established Fort de Chartres to protect the Illinois country of New France. The original wooden fort was built by Pierre Dugué de Boisbriant and was strategically located on the Mississippi River between two villages—Cahokia to the north and Kaskaskia to the south. It established civil, military, and marine government authority of the Illinois Territory and helped pursue economic goals to facilitate the fur trade, to kick-start lead mining, and to develop regional agriculture.

Soon afterward, the settlements of Saint-Philippe, Prairie du Rocher, and Nouvelle Chartres were established nearby, with their chapels managed by the parish of Sainte-Anne du Fort de Chartres, alternately served by the Society of Foreign Missions, the Jesuits, and Recollect missionaries. The parish of Saint Joseph in Prairie du Rocher was established after the village of Chartres disappeared shortly after 1765.

The Illinois Country became something of a "breadbasket to Louisiana," according to the *Digital Research Library of Illinois History Journal*. To better protect commerce and exchanges, the colonial administration decided a more robust military presence was required. Fort de Chartres was subsequently reconstructed a third time, in 1753, about one-half mile north of the first fort to avoid annual floods, incorporating stone perimeter walls, under the supervision of engineer Jean-Baptiste Saucier.

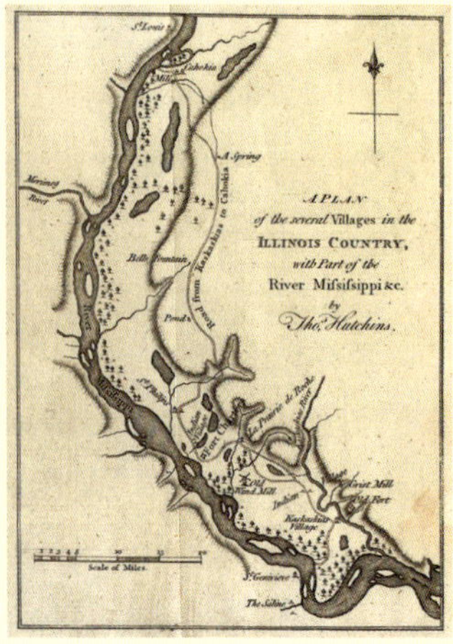

A Plan of the several Villages in the Illinois Country, with Part of the River Mississippi by Thomas Hutchins

Courtesy of David Rumsey Map Collection, David Rumsey Map Center, Stanford Libraries

Fort de Chartres, third fort erected in 1753

Drawing by John C. Guenther, FAIA, LEED LP

A New Map of the North Parts of America claimed by France under the names of Louisiana, Mississippi, Canada and New France, 1720

Drawn by Herman Moll. Courtesy of Library of Congress

1722: The Province of Louisiana

In 1722, the Province of Louisiana, under the jurisdiction of the bishop of Quebec, was divided into three sections for ecclesiastical administration. With the exception of a few Gentlemen of the Seminary in the Illinois Country, there were no diocesan priests in the whole vast territory. There were three religious orders in the Louisiana Territory serving the Indigenous missions and the French population: the Capuchins, the Discalced Carmelites, and the Jesuits. Within a few years after this division, the Carmelites were ordered back to France after having offended the Crown.

The Province of Louisiana was then divided into two sections, with the confluence of the Ohio River and the Mississippi River serving as the rough boundary. The Capuchins (the "Brown Robes") were put in charge of the southern half, to serve the Frenchmen, with New Orleans serving as their headquarters.

The Jesuits (the "Black Robes") continued their missions among the Indigenous peoples throughout the whole Mississippi River Valley and cared for the civilians in the Northern Illinois –Missouri district.

After the Jesuits offended French royalty in 1763, a royal decree ordered their expulsion from all French dominions. The expulsion of the Jesuits was a serious blow to the Church in the middle valley. The six Black Robes who had served so many of the French and the Indigenous made their way to New Orleans to join their brethren from around the world in exile.

Father Sebastien-Louis Meurin, a Jesuit priest, convinced the Superior Council to allow him to return to the Illinois Country as a non-order priest.

Of note, with the 1763 Treaty of Paris, resulting from France's loss to Great Britain in the French and Indian War (1754–63), France was stripped of her North American possessions.

Louis Bolduc House, 1793

Poteaux-sur-sole (post-on-sill) style with Norman truss roof and wraparound porch. One of the best examples of French Creole–style architecture in the United States. Photograph by John C. Guenther, FAIA, LEED AP

Green Tree Tavern, 1790

Poteaux-sur-sole (post-on-sill) style and wraparound porch. Oldest-known building in Ste. Genevieve. Photograph by John C. Guenther, FAIA, LEED AP

1735: The Middle Valley–West Bank

In the 1720s and 1730s, French interests turned to mineral deposits on the west bank of the Mississippi River in the middle valley. They discovered some fine lead outcroppings in the area, with lead mining camps springing up on the west bank, along with fertile bottom lands for farming and bountiful hunting grounds.

By 1735, the village of Ste. Genevieve, named after the patroness of Paris, was established on the west bank. Sturdy houses were built in the French Creole style of poteaux-sur-sol log cabins built with vertical logs, set five or six inches apart, with gaps filled with mud and animal hair or straw, and logs set on limestone walls, making them less likely to rot. Protective roofs were constructed of wood trusses. Covered porches wrapped the houses on all four sides to provide shade from the sun and protection from the rain, while permitting cooling breezes into the homes. Most rooms featured limestone fireplaces, while cellars below stored fruits, vegetables, and herbs.

Food was plentiful, with harvests coming from the rich soils of the Le Grand Champ—the "Big Field," including every kind of grain and vegetable: corn, pumpkins, wheat, oats, barley, flax, cotton, tobacco, yellow plums, grapes, apples, and pecans from the riverside pecan trees.

Le Vieux Village (Old Ste. Genevieve, ca. 1735) by Oscar E. Berninghaus (1924)

Mural from the Missouri State Capitol building depicting the original village settlement of Ste. Genevieve, Missouri, located on the banks of the Mississippi River. Courtesy of The State Historical Society of Missouri

Le Grand Champ served as the main common agricultural land for Old Ste. Genevieve. In addition to a house lot, each inhabitant was granted a strip of land to cultivate—approximately 192 feet wide by one mile long, set perpendicular to the Mississippi River and extending eight miles to the south to the city of St. Mary.

For many years, Father Philibert Watrin of the Jesuits of Kaskaskia crossed the river to serve the apostolic needs of the settlers in Ste. Genevieve until the early 1760s, when Father Jean-Baptiste de Lamorinie traveled from the Great Lakes region to become the first resident pastor. With the expulsion of the Jesuits by France in 1763, Ste. Genevieve was without a pastor once more.

The 1763 Treaty of Paris rewrote the map of North America.

This important map illustrated the British, Spanish, and French dominions on this great continent, exhibiting the seat of war and the French encroachments. It also illustrated all the West Indies Islands belonging to, and possessed by, the several European princes and states.

Map by Emanuel Bowen, first published ca. 1755. Courtesy of Library of Congress

1754–63: The French and Indian War

The Louisiana Territory from the Appalachians to the Rockies—including the entire Mississippi River Valley—had been controlled by France from 1699. France and Great Britain fought the French and Indian War (1754–1763), which determined control of the vast colonial territory of North America. After the British victory at the Battle of Quebec, the French surrendered Montreal to the British in 1760.

With the secret Treaty of Fontainebleau in 1762, France ceded the Louisiana Territory to Spain in the hopes of protecting their citizens and keeping the lucrative valley out of the complete control of Britain.

With the Treaty of Paris in 1763, the French and Indian War ended. France ceded Canada to Great Britain and relinquished all claims to territories east of the Mississippi River, except for New Orleans.

Many French residents living in the eastside villages of Fort de Chartres, Kaskaskia, Saint-Philippe, and Cahokia chose to move west rather than endure British rule, and they took ferries to Ste. Genevieve or St. Louis, taking with them as many of their possessions as possible.

The British victory sparked Pontiac's Rebellion (1763—64), when Native Americans grew dissatisfied with British rule and policies and attempted to drive thc British soldiers and settlers out of the Great Lakes region. The uprising by Pontiac spurred the British legislation known as the Proclamation of 1763, which created a framework for negotiating treaties with the Indigenous inhabitants of Canada and defined the North American interior west of the Appalachian Mountains as a vast Indigenous reserve.

The landing of Laclède in St. Louis. From an old print

Rozier's History of the Early Settlement of the Mississippi Valley by Firmin A. Rozier, 1890. Courtesy of The State Historical Society of Missouri–Columbia

Founding of St. Louis. Frank Nuderscher, Artist. Charles Trefts Collection, The State Historical Society of Missouri Research Center-Columbia

1763: Pierre Laclède Liguest and René-Auguste Chouteau, Jr.

On July 6, 1763, the New Orleans partnership of Maxent, Laclède & Company was granted exclusive trade rights for eight years with nations west of the Mississippi River from Jean-Jacques Blaise d'Abbadie (1726–65), the French director-general of the Colony of Louisiana. The partnership was also granted the right to establish a trading post near the confluence of the Mississippi and Missouri Rivers.

In August 1763, fur trader Pierre Laclède Liguest (1729–78) and his 14-year-old stepson, René-Auguste Chouteau, Jr., headed up the Mississippi River on board the barge *L'Esperance* with about 30 workmen and five boats stocked with trade goods and supplies. By November they arrived in Ste. Genevieve. With a lack of adequate storage space there, the group traveled on to Fort de Chartres. From there, Laclède and a small group pushed upstream to the confluence of the Mississippi and Missouri Rivers to find a suitable location. After studying the bottomlands at the confluence, the men decided against this location and navigated downstream.

In December 1763, about 18 miles south of the confluence, the exploration group found a limestone shelf on the west side of the Mississippi River. Beaching their canoes and climbing the little bluff, they looked out over wooded prairies. Laclède decided that this was to be the site of the trading post, marked several trees, and returned to Fort de Chartres. Fur trader Pierre Laclède had visited the site of what would become St. Louis.

Laclède told his stepson, Chouteau, "You will come here as soon as navigation opens, and will cause this place to be cleared, in order to form our settlement after the plan that I shall give you."

Indigenous peoples had long occupied this site. The Mississippian culture (9th–12th centuries CE) had built numerous massive earthwork mounds. St. Louis was known as "Mound City" by European Americans, given the numerous surviving prehistoric mounds, now lost to urban development.

February 15, 1764: The Founding of St. Louis

After Laclède chose the location for the trading post south of the confluence of the Mississippi and Missouri Rivers, he spent the winter of 1763 in Fort de Chartres.

In the spring of 1764, Laclède sent Chouteau ahead to start building a small settlement and trade depot. Chouteau landed at the site of what is now the St. Louis riverfront on February 14, 1764, with a troop of 21 workers and supplies. On February 15, 1764, they began to clear the site for the new city and erected buildings.

Laclède rejoined Chouteau and his workers in the spring with a detailed town plan for the settlement. It was similar to the design of New Orleans, with a grid of streets running parallel to the river. The three main north-south streets were Grande Rue, Rue de l'Eglise ("Church Street"), and Rue des Granges ("Street of Barns"). There were 18 streets perpendicular to the river. Rue de la Place (Market Street today) and Rue de la Tour (Walnut Street today) led to the central block on the riverfront—Place—used for militia drills, public assemblies, and markets. Cathedral Block (block 59) was centrally located three blocks west of the river on Rue de l'Eglise.

Pierre Laclède (1729–78)

René-Auguste Chouteau, Jr. (1749–1829)

Courtesy of Missouri Historical Society

Laclède named the settlement and fur trading post St. Louis in honor of Louis IX, King of France (1214–70). The settlement was established on French territory, although it was then legally Spanish territory after the 1763 Treaty of Paris led France to cede to Spain all of Louisiana west of the Mississippi River. There was no formal occupation by the Spanish until 1770. Several other French colonists soon moved to St. Louis.

It has been said that "Laclède founded, and Auguste Chouteau built, St. Louis."

Oscar Edward Berninghaus, American, 1874–1952; *Laclede Landing at Present Site of St. Louis,* ca..1914; oil on canvas; 22 1/2 x 44 1/2 inches. Saint Louis Art Museum, gift of August A. Busch Jr. 272:1977

1764: Cathedral Block

Colonial St. Louis grew as a commercial village and political capital, becoming a hub for trade on the Mississippi River near the confluences of the Missouri and Illinois Rivers. René-Auguste Chouteau, Jr., cofounder of St. Louis, designated the Cathedral Block in 1764 as part of the central spine of the village, including the river landing with the public square, and the Maxent, Laclède & Company Block with the fur trading house. The Catholic Church was the village's focal point for religion, civic activity, and education. On this spot was celebrated the first Mass in St. Louis in 1764. The Cathedral Block is the only plot of the colonial city that remains under the same ownership.

During the first years of its existence, St. Louis belonged to the Diocese of Quebec. In 1770, with the formal occupation of the Spanish, it became part of the Diocese of Havana.

At the time, there were only two priests in the Louisiana Territory: Father Luc Callet (1715–67), a Franciscan Recollet priest, in Cahokia; and Father Sebastien-Louis Meurin (1707–77), a former Jesuit and now a non-order priest, in Ste. Genevieve. With the passing of Father Callet in Sainte-Anne, Fort de Chartres, on September 5, 1767, Father Meurin served the spiritual needs of his widely scattered flock, from his parish in Ste. Genevieve to the east-bank parishes to St. Louis.

The very first entry in the St. Louis Parish register was made by Father Meurin in early 1766. He baptized a French infant "*en une tente, faute D'église*" (in a tent, for lack of a church). The entry, signed "S. L. Meurin, *pretre*," reported the baptism of Marie, the daughter of Jean-Baptiste Deschamps and Marie Pion, who had been born in September 1765.

In 1768, Jean-Oliver Briand, bishop of Quebec, sent the newly ordained Father Pierre Gibault to Kaskaskia. Gibault also served the French Catholics of St. Louis.

The first Catholic Church in St. Louis was built in 1770—a humble one-room log church at the northeast corner of the Cathedral Block—and was consecrated by Jesuit Father Pierre Gibault on June 24, 1770.

THE FIRST CHURCH WAS LITTLE MORE THAN A SHED

One-room log church in 1770

At the northeast corner of the Cathedral Block (1764). Consecrated by Jesuit Father Pierre Gibault on June 24, 1770. From *The Catholic Heritage of Saint Louis* by Paul Schulte (St. Louis: *The Catholic Herald*, 1934). Courtesy of Archdiocese of St. Louis Archives

1776: The Second Log Church

The official establishment of the Spanish authority in the upper reaches of Louisiana began with the arrival of Don Pedro Piernas, the first Spanish lieutenant-governor of Upper Louisiana, to St. Louis in 1770. With a change in civil authority came a change in ecclesiastical authority, and St. Louis became part of the Diocese of Havana.

The Capuchin friars were sent upriver in 1772 to care for the Catholics. Friar Valentine de Neufchâteau came to St. Louis and became the first resident priest, remaining until 1775. He offered daily Mass, regular confessions, baptisms, weddings, and funerals, and he blessed the bell of the one-room log church of 1770.

With approval on Christmas Day 1774, at a meeting at Father Valentine's residence, a new log church, 30 feet wide and 60 feet long, was to be built in the French style with vertical log walls and a broad clapboard roof with wide overhangs, at the southeast corner of Cathedral Block, facing the Rue de l'Église—Second Street. Construction began on April 19, 1775, with Pierre Lupien as carpenter. With Lupien's passing on October 18, 1775, Jean Cambas was commissioned on January 28, 1776, to complete the building, which he did shortly after the arrival of Father Bernard de Limpach in the summer of 1776.

Father Hilaire, a Capuchin stationed at Ste. Genevieve since 1773, served St. Louis following Father Valentine's departure until St. Louis received its first pastor—Father Bernard, a Capuchin, German by birth and education.

Father Bernard was formally installed on Sunday May 19, 1776, by Don Francisco Cruzat, who had replaced Piernas as lieutenant-governor in 1775 in a joyous, formal occasion —Spain's *patronato real*—the "right of royal patronage" granted to Spanish monarchs by early 16th-century popes.

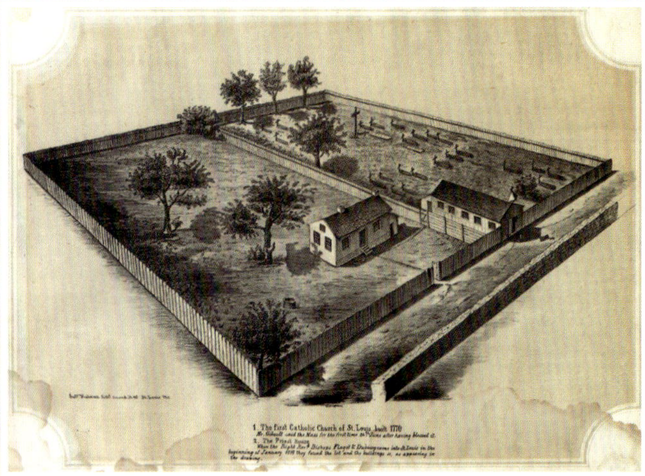

The Church of St. Louis and surrounding property in 1777

Cartographer Julius Hutawa. Undated lithograph. Courtesy of Archdiocese of St. Louis Archives

Father Bernard constructed a two-story stone residence in 1777 and 1778 to serve as the first episcopal residence alongside the log church on Cathedral Block. During his ministry of 13 years, he helped form a number of neighboring parishes, including those of St. Charles and St. Ferdinand.

From 1789 to 1793, St. Louis had no resident priest, with Reverend Mr. Ledru administering parish affairs. In 1793, Pierre-Joseph Didier, a Benedictine monk, took charge and remained until 1799.

With the arrival of the Capuchins on the west bank, the priests from the east bank ceased to cross the Mississippi River for their spiritual ministries. Father Gibault focused on tending to his flock, as he was alone after 1777. Father Sebastien Louis Meurin passed that same year and was buried in Prairie du Rocher by Father Gibault.

Pope Pius VII (r. 1800–23) reestablished the Jesuits on August 7, 1814. The Jesuits returned to the middle valley and then transferred Father Meurin's remains to the Jesuit novitiate in Florissant.

Panoramic view of St. Louis during the 1780 attack

Courtesy of Archdiocese of St. Louis Archives

Diorama of the Battle of St. Louis, Gateway Arch Museum. St. Louis, Missouri

Courtesy of the Gateway Arch National Park Archives

1780: The Battle of St. Louis and the Attack on Cahokia

Resentment for the British Empire grew in the Thirteen Colonies among colonists who desired independence as well as western expansion, forming a bond among them and pushing them toward the American Revolution to claim their nationhood on July 4, 1776.

In 1778, the Americans took the war against the British west of the Appalachian Mountains.

Lieutenant Colonel George Rogers Clark, a Virginian and older brother of William Clark, who would launch his expedition with Meriwether Lewis from St. Louis in 1804, seized control of Kaskaskia from the British. Father Gibault, assured that his Catholic flock would have freedom of religion under American rule, became a loyal backer and supporter of the patriot cause. He and the Catholic Frenchmen supported Clark, providing much needed supplies. Clark captured Fort Sackville in Vincennes on February 25, 1779, as part of the Illinois Campaign.

The land and possessions under Spain's control became targets of the British when Spain entered the war as an ally of France. The British planned a campaign in 1780 to capture St. Louis, the capital of Upper Spanish Louisiana, and control the Mississippi River corridor. British forces recruited fur traders and Indigenous tribes to join the St. Louis expedition. Emanuel Hesse commanded the force of about 50 fur traders and between 750 and 1,000 warriors.

Lieutenant Governor Fernando de Leyba received word about six weeks in advance of the pending attack from the north. With only 310 armed men under his command to defend the village, de Leyba ordered the construction of a stone tower 30 feet in diameter and 40 feet tall, with 6,000 feet of trenches extending north and south of the tower.

On April 17, 1780, pastor Father Bernard de Limpach christened the tower, blessing the foundation of the fort on the hill to the west of the church. Fort San Carlos was named in honor of His Spanish Majesty, Charles III.

Five cannons from Fort Bellefontaine on the Missouri River were mounted in the tower. Lead for muskets and cannonballs was provided by François Vallé, a former French captain from Ste. Geneveive. His two sons and 60 French militia joined in the battle. Vallé was later known as the "Defender of St. Louis."

On May 26, 1780, the British and Indigenous forces attacked St. Louis and Cahokia, landing their canoes upriver and then traveling through the woods to surprise each town. A man ran through St. Louis shouting, "To arms!" The church bell rang out to alert the citizens. The cannons of Fort San Carlos—the "Tower of Thunder"—fired a warning shot and then aimed at the hostile forces. The attackers were turned away after a two-hour battle.

George Rogers Clark arrived in Cahokia from Fort Jefferson with reinforcements of approximately 250 men, including the militia and a friendly group of Kaskaskia warriors, to help defend Cahokia and repeal the British.

The first bell to arrive in the St. Louis region hangs in the museum behind the Old Cathedral downtown. Cast in 1772 of bronze and 200 silver pieces, Father Valentine de Neufchâteau "christened" the church bell as "Pierre-Joseph Félicité" on Christmas Eve 1774. It was donated by local Spanish Lt. Gov. Benito Vasquez in honor of Lt. Gov. Pedro Joseph Piernas and Lady Piernas. Courtesy of Archdiocese of St. Louis Archives

Louisiana Purchase, 1803, and Florida Purchase, 1819

Courtesy of Library of Congress

1800–03: Louisiana Purchase

Great changes were about to unfold in America's heartland. The Church in America also faced questions of ecclesiastical authority and responsibility in the lands governed by France, Spain, Britain, and the United States.

Bishop Briand of Quebec had assumed responsibility for the Mississippi Valley and named Father Gibault as Vicar General (to Quebec) in 1768. The Vatican named Father John Carroll as Superior of the Missions in the United States in 1784. Pope Pius VI appointed Carroll as bishop of Baltimore on November 6, 1789. Carrol served from the Diocese of Baltimore with jurisdiction over the United States east of the Mississippi River. Luis Ignatius Peñalver y Cárdenas, the first bishop of the territory that became the Diocese of St. Louis, was selected as bishop of Louisiana and the Two Floridas on June 17, 1794, serving until July 20, 1801. Bishop Carroll was given jurisdiction over the Louisiana Territory in 1805. In 1808, Pope Pius VII elevated the Diocese of Baltimore to the Archdiocese of Baltimore—the first archdiocese in America, with Bishop Carroll elevated to archbishop.

Spain returned the Louisiana Territory to France as part of Napoleon's secret Third Treaty of San Ildefonso, signed on October 1, 1800. In exchange for the colony of Louisiana, Spain was to receive territories in Tuscany.

The US nominally acquired the Louisiana Territory from France for $15 million, or $18 per square mile or 3 cents per acre. A treaty was signed on May 2 but was backdated to April 30, 1803.

The US formally took possession of the Louisiana Purchase territory from France at a ceremony at the Cabildo, a government building in New Orleans, on December 20, 1803. With the transfer of the Territory of Louisiana, the US doubled its size and gained access to vast natural resources and land for new settlements, encouraging westward expansion. Importantly, the US gained control of the port of New Orleans and the Mississippi River, which was a vital trade route for the young nation.

With vague wording and ill-defined boundaries, France and the United States negotiated the Louisiana Purchase without consideration of the Indigenous tribes who had not ceded the lands where they lived to any colonial power.

"The Day of Three Flags" occurred on March 9, 1804, in St. Louis, when Lieutenant Governor de Lassus, representing Spain, officially completed the transfer of the Louisiana colonial territory to France, which then officially turned over the same lands to the United States, represented by Captain Amos Stoddard. This finalized the 1803 Louisiana Purchase and cleared the way for Lewis and Clark to begin their exploration.

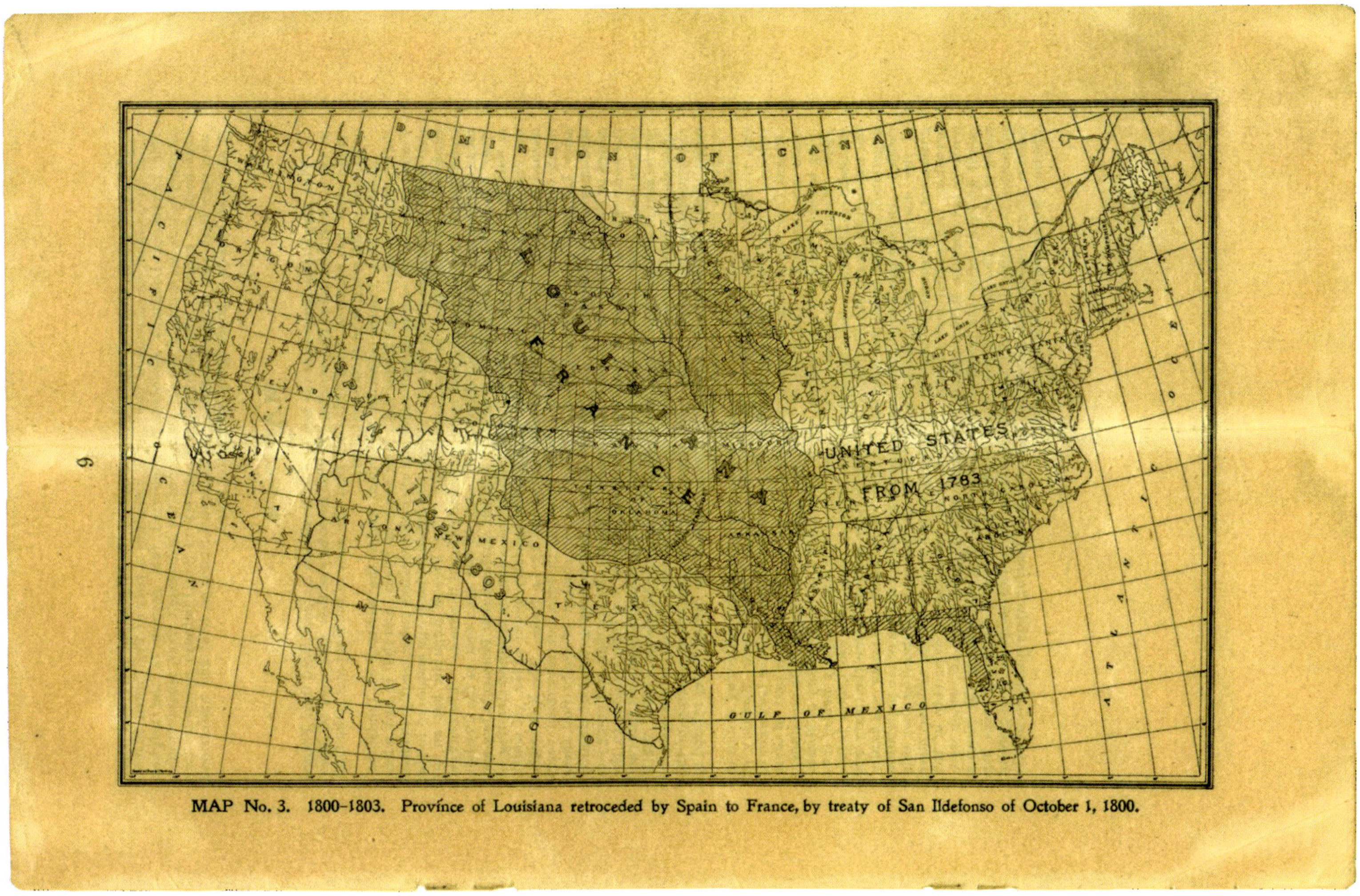

Louisiana Territory (1800–03) was retroceded by Spain to France by Treaty of San Ildefonso of October 1, 1800. Courtesy of The State Historical Society of Missouri

Postcard of a painting by F. L. Stoddard of the transfer of Upper Louisiana from France to the United States. Courtesy of Missouri Historical Society

John Carroll SJ (1735–1815)
First bishop of Baltimore

Portrait of Bishop Louis-Guillaume-Valentin DuBourg, ca. 1815

Artist Jacques Louis David (1766–1833), oil on canvas. Courtesy of the Saint Louis University Museum of Art

1812–18: Louis-Guillaume-Valentin DuBourg Arrives

Louis-Guillaume-Valentin DuBourg (1766–1833), bishop of Louisiana and the Floridas, arrived in St. Louis on January 4, 1818, on a ferry from Cahokia. A great parade was held on January 5, 1818.

To better understand the impact and importance of Bishop DuBourg's elevation to bishop of Louisiana and the Floridas, it is important to appreciate the historical context as well as DuBourg's life up to that point.

With the Louisiana Purchase of 1803, Bishop John Carroll of the Diocese of Baltimore, with jurisdiction over the United States east of the Mississippi, now had 50,000 more Catholics to serve, which doubled the size of his responsibility just as the size of the United States had doubled. He had very few clergy to help him serve this population.

Bishop Carroll named Father DuBourg as "Administrator Apostolic of the Diocese of Louisiana and the Two Floridas" on August 12, 1812. He was admitted to the Society of the Priests of Saint Sulpice. His work focused on education, and he served as president for Caroll's young foundation, which grew into Georgetown —the country's oldest Catholic university. He founded a boys' college, which became St. Mary's Seminary in Baltimore. He also served as advisor and spiritual director to Elizabeth Ann Seton when she was founding the Sisters of Charity of St. Joseph's in 1809.

DuBourg arrived in New Orleans just prior to the British army's attack on the city on January 8, 1815, in the final battle of the War of 1812. Father DuBourg and the Ursuline nuns were asked for their prayers before the battle. After the victory, at Andrew Jackson's request, DuBourg celebrated a Mass of Thanksgiving in

Elizabeth Ann Seton (1774–1821)

Foundress of the Sisters of Charity of St. Joseph's. Filicchi portrait

Courtesy of Daughters of Charity, Province of St. Louise, St. Louis, Missouri

Pope Pius VII (1742–1823)

Artist Jacques-Louis David (1805, Louvre, Paris)

the Cathedral of St. Louis (New Orleans).

At the beginning of his administration, Father DuBourg was forced to take up his residence outside New Orleans as he found the local Catholic population aligned with their pastor, Antonio de Sedella, a Capuchin monk, who rejected the jurisdiction of Bishop Carroll, an American bishop, to appoint DuBourg as administrator over the French clergy in Louisiana.

With peace coming to Louisiana, DuBourg traveled to Rome to review the situation with Pope Pius VII and seek his assistance.

On September 24, 1815, Pope Pius VII consecrated DuBourg as bishop of Louisiana and the Two Floridas in Rome, in San Luigi dei Francesi—the Church of Saint Louis of the French, which was built in 1589.

With responsibility for staffing and managing the Diocese of Louisiana, DuBourg called upon those who could be of help. While in Rome, he met Father Felix de Andreis while visiting the motherhouse of the Congregation of the Mission. Impressed with de Andreis's qualities, DuBourg asked him to be the director of a seminary he envisioned in his new diocese. Father Charles Dominic Sicardi, Lazarist superior, initially resisted this request, but with the intercession of the papal secretary of state and Pope Pius VII, he relented and assigned Father de Andreis to DuBourg's new diocese on September 27, 1815.

Father de Andreis then turned to his fellow Lazarist, Father Joseph Rosati, a former pupil of his, making him de Andreis's first recruit. Others volunteered to become priests in America and received the blessings of Pope Pius VII. Arrangements were made while books, religious articles, and funds were gathered for the missions in America.

Pauline Jaricot (1799–1862)

Foundress, The Society for the Propagation of the Faith

Courtesy of Pontifical Missionaries of France

Mother Rose Philippine Duchesne (1769–1852), Society of the Sacred Heart

Courtesy of the Society of the Sacred Heart

1812–18: Recruiting Missionaries

In 1815, while in Lyons, France, Bishop DuBourg collected alms for his diocese. He met with Madame Petit, who had once lived in Baltimore, and suggested founding a charitable association for the support of Louisiana missions. He won her favor and financial support. Separately, the Society for the Propagation of the Faith was founded in 1822 by Pauline Jaricot (1799–1862), who had been collecting for missions since 1818.

DuBourg had encountered resistance to his authority at the diocesan seat of New Orleans. While in Europe, he wrote a letter to the Congregation of the Propaganda Fide in Rome, asking to establish his new episcopal see in St. Louis, hoping to avoid conflict with and stay far away from the tumultuous New Orleans.

While in Paris, on May 16, 1816, DuBourg appealed to Mother Madeleine Sophie Barat, foundress of the Society of the Sacred Heart, for nuns to work in the United States. Mother Philippine Duchesne had pleaded for an assignment as a missionary to serve the Native Americans, which was granted by Mother Barat. In 1818, she headed a group of four bound for St. Louis. She was named "the woman who always prays" by the Potawatomi she served.

DuBourg's recruited missionaries set sail from Bordeaux on the *Ranger* on June 12, 1816, while DuBourg remained in Europe. They arrived in Baltimore on July 26, 1816.

Father de Andreis and his missionaries traveled from Baltimore to the seminary in Bardstown, Kentucky, the city of Bishop Benedict Joseph Flaget, arriving there on November 19, 1816. Another delegation, many of them nuns, sailed to New Orleans, reaching the Ursuline convent on January 3, 1817.

Felix de Andreis, CM (1778–1820)

Reproduction of the painting, oil on canvas, ca. 1820, in the Collegio Leoniano, Rome. Rev. Felix de Andreis, CM, personnel files, Box 5. Vincentian Archives, Special Collections and Archives, DePaul University Library, Chicago, Illinois

Right Reverend Joseph Rosati, CM (1789–1843), ca. 1843

Artist unknown. Oil on canvas. Courtesy of the Congregation of the Mission House in Rome, Italy. The painting is preserved at Collegio Apostolico Leoniano in Rome.

As DuBourg continued his begging for the diocese, he received more funds, articles, and artwork, which one can view in the Old Cathedral of St. Louis today!

On July 1, 1817, DuBourg set sail from Bordeaux on *La Caravane*, a ship provided by the King of France, the Bourbon Louis XVIII, with a group of 29 men, including five more priests, 13 seminarians, three Brothers of the Christian Schools, four students about to enter seminary training, and four lay volunteers. They arrived on September 4, 1817, in Annapolis, with DuBourg traveling on to Baltimore and St. Mary's Seminary.

Bishop DuBourg and his group left Baltimore on November 4, 1817, to reunite with Father de Andreis and his group of missionaries and seminarians in Bardstown. They then traveled to Louisville, boarding the steamboat *Piqua* to St. Louis. With winter setting in and rivers freezing, they reached Apple Creek on the west side of the Mississippi River and proceeded to Ste. Genevieve, arriving on December 31, 1817, with Bishop DuBourg celebrating a Pontifical High Mass on January 1, 1818.

The group traveled from Ste. Genevieve to Cahokia. The bishops boarded an awaiting ferryboat, which transported them to St. Louis, where 2,500 inhabitants greeted them on the riverfront on January 5, 1818.

The bishops were led in a joyous procession to the rectory, where they dressed in miters and episcopal robes, and along with 12 altar boys, processed on the Rue de l'Eglise to the church—a vertical log building from 1776, where the Episcopal chair was prepared for Bishop Flaget to conduct the official ceremony of installation of Bishop DuBourg, commending him to his diocese.

1818: The Brick Church

It became obvious to Bishop DuBourg that the second log church (1776) should be replaced.

On January 8, 1818, just three days after his installation, he wrote, "My Cathedral is a kind of miserable barn falling in ruins, which makes it imperative for me to build another church." Father de Andreis reinforced this thought, writing on February 24, 1818, "We have nothing now to serve the purpose of a church, but a miserable log-cabin, open to every wind and falling in pieces." Icy blasts were known to blow through the chinks between the vertical logs in the walls.

By January 8, 1818, DuBourg announced the new church would measure 150 feet in length and 70 feet in width. Such certainty was made possible by a visit to St. Louis in the fall of 1817 by Bishop Benedict Joseph Flaget of Kentucky to discuss the site, size, and materials of the new church, along with establishing financial subscriptions to raise funds. The list of subscribers was a who's who of early St. Louis families.

The new church, designed by Gabriel Paul, was located on the northeast corner of the property, over a portion of the existing cemetery, at the corner of Second Street and Market Street. Ground was broken early in 1818 and foundations started at once. DuBourg laid the cornerstone on March 29, 1818, at 4 p.m. By April 20, 1818, the exterior walls were 6 feet high. By July, those walls were about 15 feet high. The cathedral was under roof by mid-November 1818. Its middle nave measured 134 feet in length and 40 feet in width. The five large arches on each side, originally planned to separate the middle from the side aisles, were infilled with brick, with planned side aisles never constructed. The arches were filled in temporarily so the building could be used for the first services. The Panic of 1819 resulted in a cessation of fundraising needed to complete the building.

Bishop DuBourg had to wait until January 9, 1820, to formally dedicate the church with a solemn blessing.

Brick church (1818–19) (burned 1835). Designed by Gabriel Paul at the request of Reverend Bishop DuBourg

Courtesy of Archdiocese of St. Louis Archives

Despite its meager proportion, the new brick church held sacred vases, ornaments, and artworks—original paintings by Rubens, Raphael, Guido, and Paul Veronese—along with ancient and precious gold embroideries, all thanks to the generosity of European Catholics, including Louis XVIII (King of France) and Baroness La Candale de Ghyseghem of Belgium, who presented these to Bishop DuBourg on his last visit through France, Italy, Sicily, and the Netherlands.

With the new church completed, the cathedral block now contained extensive gardens, a grape arbor, a stable, a refectory, two wells, a bathhouse, a cemetery, the bishop's home, and a college building—Saint Louis Academy, predecessor of Saint Louis University—to which DuBourg pledged his personal library of 8,000 volumes. It opened in November 1818, with classes in Latin, English, French, arithmetic, mathematics, and geography. Enlarged boarding facilities were added by the fall of 1820. The school offered its first adult evening classes. October 15, 1820, marked the passing of the school's first professor of prominence, Father de Andreis.

The Saint Louis Academy (1818–32), later St. Mary's Chapel (1832), to the south of the brick church (dedicated 1820) on Cathedral Block

Cartographer Julius Hutawa. Courtesy of Archdiocese of St. Louis Archives

St. Ferdinand's Convent (1819) and Church (1821), Florissant, Missouri

Photograph by John C. Guenther, FAIA, LEED AP

1818–26: The Academies

1818 was a year of significant growth and impact for religious education and formation in the Diocese of Louisiana and the Two Floridas under Bishop DuBourg's leadership.

In 1818, he announced the plans and began construction for a proper cathedral on Cathedral Block, as well as a Catholic university—the Saint Louis Academy, the first west of the Mississippi River.

On March 31, 1818, two days after laying the cornerstone for his brick cathedral in St. Louis, Bishop DuBourg headed to Perryville, some 80 miles south of St. Louis, to establish a theological seminary and college at "The Barrens" in 1818. The Vincentians built St. Mary's of the Barrens on 640 acres of fertile land—the first Catholic seminary in American territory west of the Mississippi River. Father Joseph Rosati moved to Perryville and planned and supervised the construction of the school, while also teaching most of the classes and functioning as the local pastor. St. Mary's Seminary was incorporated in 1822.

In March of 1818, 47-year-old Mother Rose Philippine Duchesne and four sisters, with the blessing of Mother Barat and at the invitation of Bishop DuBourg, departed France for their missionary work in the New World. Mother Duchesne was tasked with building a school in the frontier town of St. Charles. On September 14, 1818, she opened the Academy of the Sacred Heart in the Duquette Mansion, the first tuition-free school west of the Mississippi River. By 1819, Mother Duchesne and the Society of the Sacred Heart relocated to Florissant, Missouri, near St. Ferdinand Church for the purpose of establishing a girls' school.

In 1820, Mother Duchesne opened the first novitiate. Six other schools soon followed in Missouri and Louisiana. In 1828, the sisters returned to reopen the school in St. Charles.

In 1819, the Academy of Ste. Genevieve became the first school in the western hemisphere taught by three Christian Brothers, sent under King Louis XVIII. It grew out of the Old Louisiana Academy, founded 1808, the first school in the United States west of the Mississippi.

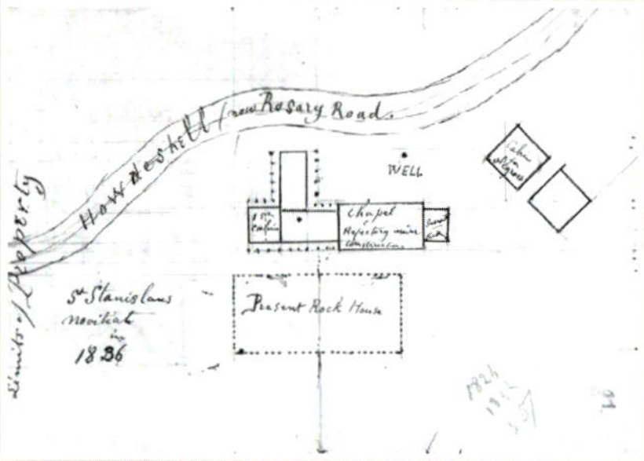

St. Stanislaus Novitiate, Florissant, Missouri
Buildings include "1st Cabin." 1836 map
Courtesy Jesuit Archives & Research Center

St. Stanislaus Novitiate
Site of the St. Regis Indian Seminary, opened May 11, 1824, in Florissant, Missouri. Courtesy Jesuit Archives & Research Center

1818–26: The American Mission and St. Regis Seminary / St. Stanislaus Novitiate

Father Charles Nerinckx (1761–1824) eventually decided to emigrate to America in 1804 when the army of the French Republic invaded Belgium in 1797, persecuting Catholic priests. Bishop John Carroll accepted his services for the American mission in Kentucky. With a focus on Catholic education, Nerinckx founded the Loretto Sisters as a teaching order in 1812, based in the rural community of Nerinx, Kentucky. DuBourg also invited the Sisters of Loretto to establish a school for girls.

During a trip to Europe to obtain supplies, Father Nerinckx persuaded Pierre-Jean De Smet (1801–73) to join the American mission. In 1821, Father Nerinckx set sail for America on the brig *Mars* with De Smet, Henry Verhaegaen, and ten other Belgian Jesuits who intended to become missionaries to Native Americans. They arrived at the Jesuit novitiate at Whitemarsh, Maryland, near Baltimore.

In 1818, Bishop DuBourg acquired 212 acres of ground in the common fields of Florissant. In 1823, DuBourg made an agreement with the Superior of the Society of Jesus in the United States to bring a group of Jesuits from White Marsh, Maryland, to Florissant. Shortly thereafter, DuBourg conveyed "Bishop's Farm" to the Jesuit Order for the purpose of establishing a seminary.

On April 11, 1823, De Smet and five other Belgian novices, led by novice master Charles Van Quickenborne, traveled to Florissant at the invitation of Bishop DuBourg to complete his theological studies and to begin his studies of Native American languages. On January 7, 1824, DuBourg offered the Jesuits control of the Saint Louis Academy, which had become known as Saint Louis College in 1820.

De Smet was ordained a priest on September 23, 1827, at the Shrine of St. Ferdinand (built 1821). The Jesuits founded several academic institutions, among which was the St. Regis Indian Seminary, where De Smet had his first contacts with Indigenous students. He learned about various tribal customs and languages while serving as a prefect at the seminary.

The St. Regis Seminary, a local boarding school and the only Catholic Indian school in the United States at this time, opened on May 11, 1824, in Florissant, Missouri. Beginning with five Indigenous boys, it grew to 30 before closing in 1831. St. Stanislaus Novitiate occupied the same site. Originally intended by DuBourg to "familiarize" his young missionaries with "their manners and languages" and to educate and convert Indigenous children, their treatment has recently come to light, with research into Native American boarding schools and reconciliation underway.

Map of the Diocese of St. Louis in 1826

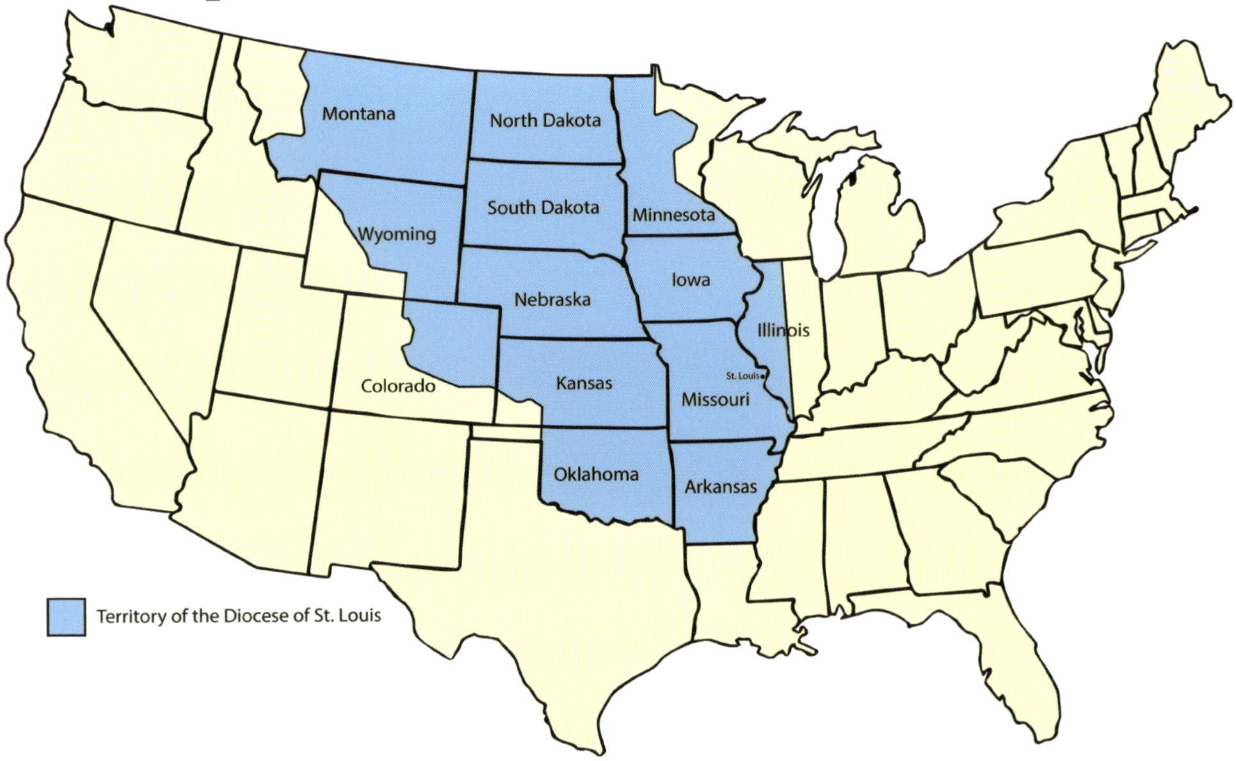

Map of the Original Diocese of St. Louis, 1826. Courtesy of Archdiocese of St. Louis Office of Archives and Records

July 18, 1826: Original Diocese of Saint Louis

Bishop DuBourg, along with Mother Duchesne and her Society of the Sacred Heart, Father Van Quickenborne and his Jesuits, and Father Rosati and his Vincentians in St. Mary's of the Barrens, contributed to laying the foundation that would make St. Louis "The Rome of the West."

In 1823, Father Rosati was appointed coadjutor bishop to Bishop DuBourg for the dioceses of Louisiana and the Floridas. This allowed Bishop DuBourg to return to New Orleans to make his residence there, while Rosati was based in St. Louis.

In 1826, Bishop DuBourg traveled to the Holy See in Rome. Reluctant to enforce his authority against the cathedral trustees who continually opposed him, he tendered his resignation of the See of New Orleans, believing another incumbent would be more successful.

Pope Leo XII then divided the Louisiana Territory into two dioceses—New Orleans and St. Louis—thus founding the Diocese of St. Louis on July 18, 1826.

Right Reverend Joseph Rosati, first bishop of St. Louis. Artist Louis Schultze, 1887. Courtesy of Missouri Historical Society

Pope Leo XII (1760–1829)
Artist Charles Picqué, 1828

Pope Leo XII appointed Joseph Rosati, CM (1789–1843) as the apostolic administrator of both dioceses on July 18, 1826. Rosati was then appointed the first bishop of St. Louis on March 20, 1827.

The Diocese of St. Louis covered half of the country.

St. Louis Mullanphy Hospital, which was founded in 1828, was the first hospital established west of the Mississippi River. The building shown in the image was from 1874. Photographer Henry Richard Fuhrmann. Courtesy of Missouri Historical Society

1828–32: Hospitals, Orphanages, Deaf Education, and Higher Education

At the request of Bishop DuBourg, the Sisters of Charity arrived by stagecoach to St. Louis in November 1828. Their successful works led to opening the St. Louis Mullanphy Hospital in 1831 on Spruce Street between Third and Fourth Streets—the first hospital west of the Mississippi. John Mullanphy provided the property, plus $350 to purchase furnishings and $150 traveling money, and stipulated the hospital must care for "all such indigent sick free persons without regard to color, country, or religion." They cared for many poor people and the victims of the great cholera epidemic of 1832. In 1873–74, the St. Louis Mullanphy Hospital relocated to Montgomery Street and Bacon Street, just east of Grand Avenue.

The Sisters of Charity also opened the first Catholic orphanage for boys in the state of Missouri with Mullanphy donating property and funds for the orphanage adjacent to Mullanphy Hospital. In 1834, the St. Louis Male Orphan

Saint Louis University, 1832, Washington Ave. to Christy Ave., 9th St. to 11th St. Aerial view looking west

Courtesy of Saint Louis University Archives

Saint Louis University, 1841. Street-level view looking north

Courtesy of Saint Louis University Archives

Asylum was established next to the Old Cathedral at Third and Walnut Streets and put in the hands of the Sisters of Charity. By 1835 there were 46 orphaned boys at the home.

In 1829, the Jesuits assumed control of Saint Louis College, and Father Peter Verhaegen was named to succeed Van Quickenborne as the fourth president of the college. The Jesuit college opened to the west of the riverfront with their campus located at Washington Avenue and 9th Street in 1829. Father Verhaegen became the first president of Saint Louis University, serving from 1829 to 1836. On December 28, 1832, Missouri Governor Daniel Dunkin signed the charter bill by the Missouri General Assembly that made Saint Louis University the first university west of the Mississippi. Father Verhaegen oversaw construction of the university's first permanent building, along with forming its curriculum. Within a few years the rapidly growing university added a medical college.

Mother St. John Fontbonne, superior of the Sisters of St. Joseph in France, responded to a request for teachers by Bishop Rosati, who hoped to establish an institute for the deaf. A wealthy French woman, Countess de la Rochejacquelin, an influential noblewoman who greatly admired the Sisters of St. Joseph, agreed to finance their journey to the distant missions of Missouri. In 1836, six sisters made the arduous journey from the motherhouse in Lyon, France, to the villages of Carondelet and Cahokia. Three sisters established their little congregation on a bluff overlooking the Mississippi River. The location is still the motherhouse of the order today at 6400 Minnesota. In March 1837, two more sisters arrived. They were specially trained to teach deaf children, many of whom had lost their hearing to diphtheria and scarlet fever. Within a few years at Carondelet, the sisters established a coed school for young children, the St. Joseph Institute for the Deaf, and in 1840, St. Joseph's Academy, an elementary and secondary school for girls. Their shoestring budget required great sacrifice and the aid of generous benefactors.

1831–34: The Cathedral of St. Louis (Old Cathedral)

It has been said the Church of St. Louis (built 1818) was called a cathedral only by courtesy. Now, with the founding of the Archdiocese of St. Louis on July 18, 1826, St. Louis deserved a true cathedral. As Bishop Rosati wrote of the 1818 church, "only half-finished, rather rustic inside, and looking much like a hay barn," it had been poorly built with one of its side walls in danger of collapse. With a debt cleared after several years of effort, the cost of the needed repairs would be great, without any improvement to the building's appearance. Given the rapid growth of St. Louis, it was felt that the city should have a cathedral in keeping with its needs and dignity. After lengthy deliberation of the circumstances, Rosati made the decision to build a new cathedral.

The Cathedral of St. Louis (Old Cathedral) was built 1831–34, to the design of Joseph Lavielle & George Morton, architects—the first architectural firm west of the Mississippi. The cathedral design—a prominent example of Greek Revival architecture—was to be 136 feet long, 84 feet wide, and 40 feet tall. Its stone facade was made of Joliet stone from Joliet, Illinois, and featured four Doric-style columns, 27 feet tall and 4 feet in diameter, supporting a pediment, forming a 40-foot-long and 12-foot-deep portico. A 20-foot square, 40-foot-high belfry, and 45-foot-tall octagonal steeple rise above.

The first stone was blessed and set on Sunday evening, August 1, 1831, by Bishop Rosati. Completed in 1834, the cathedral was dedicated on October 26, 1834. This is the first building of national significance built in the state and the first cathedral west of the Mississippi River. It is a very early example of Greek Revival architecture with many Federal elements remaining, as noted in Talbot Hamlin's book, *Greek Revival Architecture in America* (1944).

In 1845, the First Conference of the Society of St. Vincent de Paul in the United States was organized here at this venerable cathedral.

The Cathedral of St. Louis (Old Cathedral)

Wood engraving by J. T. Hammond after J. C. Wild, 1840. Courtesy of Missouri Historical Society

1840–43: "Don't Disturb the Lion."

From May 7, 1839, to October 19, 1839, Bishop Rosati made a grand tour of the diocese he had shepherded for 13 years. St. Louis had grown to between 35,000 and 40,000 residents, with 40 to 50 percent Catholic. French, English, Creole, and German parishioners all wanted sermons in their native languages. The diocese was far from wealthy, with debts amounting to $60,000. Rosati was frugal in building the cathedral, proceeding without marble altars and stained glass windows, while keeping careful records of every transaction.

On December 8, 1839, he approved the establishment of the St. Vincent de Paul Society Chapter in St. Louis—the first in America—for Catholic laity to serve the poor.

In April 1840, Rosati decided he must travel to Rome to present the condition of his diocese to the Propaganda Fide and Pope Gregory XVI. Before leaving St. Louis, Rosati wrote his will and named Father Verhaegen as executor. En route, Bishop Rosati attended the Fourth Provincial Council of Baltimore and then proceeded to Philadelphia, where he was a guest of Bishop Francis Patrick Kenrick. While there, he renewed his acquaintance with Vicar-General Peter Richard Kenrick, younger brother of Bishop Kenrick. This meeting led Bishop Rosati to ask Pope Gregory XVI to name Peter Richard Kenrick as his coadjutor of the Diocese of St. Louis.

On September 17, 1840, Bishop Rosati, along with other Vincentians, had a private audience with Pope Gregory XVI at Castel Gandolfo, followed by a nearly two-hour private conversation between the Pope and Rosati. In further discussions in Rome, the Pope agreed that Father Kenrick of Philadelphia should be Rosati's coadjutor. The Pope also asked Rosati to negotiate a concordat in Haiti.

Bishop Rosati returned to America in the fall of 1841. On November 30, 1841, he consecrated Peter Richard Kenrick, just 35 years of age, as bishop and coadjutor of the Diocese of St. Louis.

Portrait of Archbishop Peter Richard Kenrick (1806–96)
Artist unknown, ca. 1850. Courtesy of Archdiocese of St. Louis Archives

Bishop Rosati traveled to Port-au-Prince to negotiate the concordat, which was signed. Rosati then sailed to Europe in April 1842 to review his efforts in Rome with Vatican officials. Rosati's health began to fail, and on September 25, 1843, at the age of 54, he died. He was buried at Monte Citorio.

After serving a year and a half as coadjutor, Peter Richard Kenrick was named ordinary and bishop of the St. Louis Diocese upon the death of Bishop Rosati. Kenrick's episcopacy would be the longest in St. Louis history. His episcopal motto was *"Noli irritare leonem"*—translated, "Don't disturb the lion." Kenrick would be a lion for Catholic religious liberty, a lion in his church and in his city.

View of interior and altar, ca. 1890, the Cathedral of St. Louis (Old Cathedral)

Photographer E. Boehl. Courtesy of Archdiocese of St. Louis Archives

Ruins of the Great St. Louis Fire, May 17–18, 1849

Photographer Thomas Easterly. Courtesy of Missouri Historical Society

1847–64: St. John the Apostle and Evangelist, Pro-Cathedral

In 1847, the growing diocese of St. Louis became an archdiocese. On July 20, 1847, Bishop Peter Richard Kenrick became the first archbishop in St. Louis history. St. John the Apostle and Evangelist Parish was founded in 1847 to serve Catholics moving west of the original city of St. Louis. The area had been a peach orchard.

In 1849, St. Louis experienced the Great Fire, the return of cholera, and anti-Irish riots fanned by the Native American Party, colloquially referred to as the "Know Nothings."

The Great St. Louis Fire began about 10 p.m. on May 17, 1849, on board the *White Cloud* steamboat, moored near the head of the levee on the St. Louis riverfront, when it caught fire and sank in its moorings. Fanned by a strong wind that blew from the northeast, the fire spread rapidly downriver lighting up the whole line of boats along the levee and into St. Louis, claiming 23 steamboats, 430 buildings on 15 riverfront city blocks, and three lives. With the entire business district of the city apparently doomed, a group of volunteer firemen exploded several businesses in succession in front of the fire with kegs of black powder. Tragically, Captain Thomas B. Targee of Missouri Company No. 5 died while the powder he was spreading exploded prematurely. His heroic actions preserved the Old Cathedral.

In 1853, the vision for the Old Cathedral was finally completed under the direction of Archbishop Kenrick with extensive alterations to the interior of the church, fulfilling Bishop Rosati's original plan.

In 1860, St. John the Apostle and Evangelist Church was completed and dedicated on November 4, 1860. After the Civil War, Archbishop Kenrick adopted St. John the Apostle and Evangelist Church as his cathedral and residence, preferring to move away from the crowded St. Louis riverfront and the Old Cathedral, as he felt it was no longer adequate in size and its location had become undesirable. In 1864, it was elevated to Pro-Cathedral (1864–1914). The archbishop's residence was located across the main plaza of the church, on what was then 16th Street.

St. John the Apostle and Evangelist Pro-Cathedral, 16th and Chestnut Streets, interior, St. Louis, Missouri

Courtesy of St. Louis Globe-Democrat Collection, from the collections at the St. Louis Mercantile Library at the University of Missouri–St. Louis

1870s–80s: St. Louis Moves Westward

Most Rev. Peter Richard Kenrick (1806–96)

Coadjutor of St. Louis (1841–43)

Bishop of St. Louis (1843–47)

Archbishop of St. Louis (1847–95)

Courtesy of Archdiocese of St. Louis Archives

Within the city there were some 250,000 Catholics, growing from the original Catholic census of 8,601 made by the episcopal authority. From Eleventh Street to the west, and Rutger Street to the south, the boundary line of the city moved west to Eighteenth Street and south to Louisa Street in 1841. In 1870, the boundaries extended beyond Grand Avenue and south to include Carondelet. By 1876, the city's boundary was established further west and to the north.

The Cathedral of St. Louis (Old Cathedral), on the *Rue de l'Eglise*—Second Street—was now surrounded by the businesses of the riverfront. Early St. Louis families—the Maffits, Sarpys, Popes, Filleys, Reyburns, Lucases, Soulards, Bertholds, Vallés, Benoists, and the Chéniers—had abandoned their homes, moving further west, giving way to modern office buildings and industries. The social and commercial life shifted westward with each passing year. The Old Cathedral, with its stately Doric columns and quiet grandeur, remained a witness to history, past and present, while the neighborhood became cramped and commercial.

Planning for the new cathedral began under the authority of Archbishop Peter Richard Kenrick in the 1870s and 1880s. A formal organization promoting the new cathedral was created on April 28, 1871. Members of the St. Louis Cathedral Building Association included Archbishop Kenrick, Bishop Patrick John Ryan, and a variety of local businessmen.

The Old St. Louis Cathedral. Walnut Street between Second and Third Streets

From *The Notable Catholic Institutions of St. Louis and Vicinity* by Francis A. Thornton (1911). Courtesy of St. Louis Public Library–Central Library

Archbishop Kenrick secured a site near Eighteenth and Locust Streets, but before the project could be started, the city had leapt a half mile to the west. A second site, seven blocks further west on the southeast corner of Jefferson Avenue and Locust Street, was given by Mrs. Anna Lucas Hunt. Before the prelate was ready to begin the work, the center of population had shifted again. A location near Grand Avenue was thought to be more suitable but later abandoned. Delay upon delay, coupled with a financial depression, and waiting to see how far the city population might expand westward all contributed to a pause in realizing the New Cathedral.

Sadly, on March 4, 1896, Archbishop Kenrick "had to go to his rest robbed of that crowning glory which he had so long hoped to achieve for the great Master he loved so well."

St. Louis Cathedral Chapel (1896)

Maryland and Newstead Avenues

From *Notable Catholic Institutions* (1911). Courtesy of St. Louis Public Library–Central Library

Most Rev. John J. Kain (1843–1903)

Coadjutor of St. Louis (1893–95)

Archbishop of St. Louis (1895–1903)

Courtesy of Archdiocese of St. Louis Archives

Pictured Story of the Tornado. Published by *Southern Age*, St. Louis, Missouri

Great Western Ptg. Co., St. Louis, Missouri, p. 45 Church of St. John of Nepomuk, Soulard and Eleventh Streets; p. 48 Church of Sts. Peter and Paul, Seventh Street and Allen Avenue

1893–96: A Site for the New Cathedral

In 1895, Archbishop Kenrick was canonically deposed by Pope Leo XIII because of physical incapacitation due to infirmity. On June 16, 1893, Bishop John J. Kain (1843–1903) was decreed by Rome as coadjutor archbishop (successor) of the Diocese of St. Louis. He arrived in St. Louis from Wheeling, West Virginia, in 1893. On June 8, 1895, Kain was installed as Archbishop of St. Louis—the first American-born archbishop of the city, with a diocese of 354 priests and a Catholic population of 200,000.

On September 21, 1893, Archbishop Kain presided at the reopening of the philosophy and theology departments of the Archdiocesan Seminary. The new seminary, located in a former convent of the Visitation Nuns, at 19th Street and Cass Avenue in St. Louis, was the first site to bear the name Kenrick Seminary. Once again, the seminary was entrusted to the direction of the Vincentian Community.

Archbishop Kain carried on with the work of finding a suitable site for the New Cathedral. Two pieces of property were considered: one at the southwest corner of McPherson and Taylor Avenues, the other fronting Lindell Boulevard, with Newstead Avenue to the east and Maryland Avenue to the north. Archbishop Kain selected the second option, purchased the property in 1895 for $100,000, and had design sketches prepared for the New Cathedral. He prepared plans for funding and raised $200,000.

In 1896, Archbishop Kain had the New Cathedral Chapel built on the corner of Maryland and Newstead Avenues. He made this church his Pro-Cathedral, serving as such until the completion of the New Cathedral. The Cathedral Chapel was blessed on October 18, 1896, by the first pastor, Reverend J. McCaffrey.

The catastrophic tornado of May 27, 1896, tore through the south side of St. Louis, killing hundreds and severely damaging the city and many churches, such as St. Frances de Sales, St. Patrick, St. John Nepomuk, and Saints Peter and Paul. The property loss reached a half million dollars, delaying the New Cathedral project while the Diocese of St. Louis repaired the damaged churches.

Barnett, Haynes & Barnett, architects, Cathedral of Saint Louis

Courtesy of Archdiocese of St. Louis Archives

THE REPUBLIC: SUNDAY, JUNE 9, 1901.

NEW CATHOLIC CATHEDRAL IN LINDELL BOULEVARD.

ACCEPTED PLAN FOR THE NEW CATHOLIC CATHEDRAL AT NEWSTEAD AVENUE AND LINDELL BOULEVARD.

Accepted plan for the new Catholic cathedral at Newstead Avenue and Lindell Boulevard

From *St. Louis Republic,* June 9, 1901. Courtesy of Missouri Historical Society

1901: The First Design

Archbishop John J. Kain dedicated his efforts to realize the new St. Louis cathedral. He wrote a pastoral letter to the people of the Archdiocese, "but all admit that the new St. Louis should have another—more handsome and more worthy [cathedral] . . . of the great Catholic city of the West."

The planning and design of the New Cathedral in the style of the Roman Basilica were described in the *St. Louis Republic* of June 9, 1901, noting that "The building represents, in fact, the matured thought of His Grace, the Archbishop, who has, with his architects, Barnett, Haynes & Barnett, for the last two years studiously collaborated on the problem, which, as represented, embodies the ideas gathered both here and abroad, and when finished the structure will be one that not alone the Catholic community, but the entire city, can point to with pride, as, in comparison with others, as to cost and design, it will be second to none in this country."

The design called for a plan 90 feet wide and 240 feet long, with transepts 100 feet wide and a dome of 225 feet in height. The entry facade featured three portals beneath a pediment 90 feet above, flanked by two towers disengaged from the main building.

The article went on to say, "The interior as designed will be on a scale more elegant even than that of the exterior. . . . A special feature of the interior will be the lighting effects produced by concealed electric lights, emphasizing the cornices, arches, niches, and other architectural effects of the interior of the building and dome, when required for grand ceremonial."

The St. Louis architectural firm of Barnett, Haynes & Barnett was founded about 1895 by Thomas P. Barnett, John Ignatius Haynes, and George Dennis Barnett. The Barnetts were sons of English-born St. Louis architect George I. Barnett, and Haynes was George D. Barnett's brother-in-law.

George I. Barnett (1815–98) came to St. Louis from Nottingham, England, in 1839. As one of St. Louis's first professionally trained architects, he was known as "The Dean of Architects." His architectural legacy includes St. Vincent DePaul Church in LaSalle Park (1844-45), the Grand Avenue Water Tower (1871), Henry Shaw´s Country House (1849)—"Tower Grove House," the Henry Shaw Mausoleum (1889) at the Missouri Botanical Garden, and the Missouri Governor's Mansion (1871).

1903–04: Bold Visions

Archbishop Kain asked the Holy Father to appoint Irish-born John J. Glennon (1862–1946), coadjutor bishop of Kansas City, to be his coadjutor archbishop of St. Louis, so named on April 27, 1903.

Glennon succeeded Archbishop Kain as the fourth archbishop of St. Louis upon the latter's death on October 13, 1903. Providing significant leadership to the Diocese of St. Louis, Archbishop Glennon set about planning and building the great New Cathedral of Saint Louis on the site that Archbishop Kain had chosen at Lindell Boulevard and Newstead Avenue. Although Archbishop Kain went to his grave without realizing the great cathedral, he made the cathedral the beneficiary of his personal property at the time of his death.

The Louisiana Purchase Exposition—the 1904 St. Louis World's Fair—brought the world to St. Louis. It featured an amazing array of impressive buildings dramatically set within what is Forest Park today.

One such building was the Palace of Liberal Arts, covering nine acres. It was designed in a French Renaissance style by George D. Barnett of the architectural firm of Barnett, Haynes & Barnett, who had submitted the design of the New Cathedral in 1901 after collaborating with Archbishop Kain for two years.

Archbishop John J. Glennon (1862–1946), ca. 1903

Courtesy of Archdiocese of St. Louis Archives

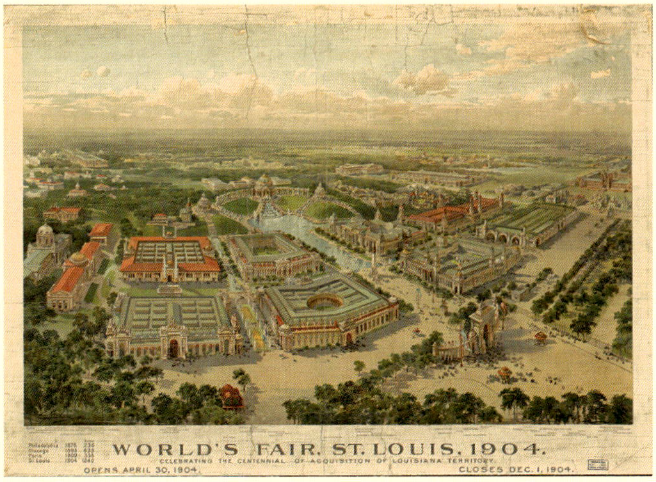

St. Louis World's Fair, 1904 Louisiana Purchase Exposition, celebrating the centennial of the acquisition of Louisiana Territory. ca. 1903

Courtesy of Library of Congress

Archbishop John J. Glennon with Apostolic Delegate at 1904 World's Fair

Courtesy of the Archdiocese of St. Louis Office of Archives and Records

The New St. Louis Cathedral, side elevation, Newstead Avenue

From *Notable Catholic Institutions* (1911). Courtesy of St. Louis Public Library–Central Library

The New St. Louis Cathedral, front elevation, Lindell Boulevard

From *The Notable Catholic Institutions of Saint Louis and Vicinity* (1911)

1905: A Competition

Archbishop John Joseph Glennon revived the plans for the new cathedral in his epoch-making sermon on February 5, 1905. "From the first day I came amongst you, I found pressing on me with ever-increasing urgency this great work, the fulfillment of which is evidently the will of God . . . I propose to build a temple in the name of the Lord my God." (1 Kings 5:19)

On May 14, 1905, James Cardinal Gibbons, archbishop of Baltimore, came to St. Louis to bestow on Archbishop Glennon the pallium and symbols of his office in a ceremony at the Old Cathedral on the St. Louis riverfront. On this occasion, Archbishop John Ireland of Saint Paul insisted that the new cathedral go forward, urging Archbishop Glennon, "Build your cathedral!"

In ceremonies that followed, the priests of the archdiocese gave Archbishop Glennon $60,000 from their own funds, which quickly reached $71,200 with a gift from R. C. Kerens, a railroad investor. Thirty-two lay members subscribed another $250,000.

In the summer of 1905, Archbishop Glennon wanted to solicit new design concepts for the new cathedral and devised a competition program of 19 pages for a million-dollar church. Firms submitting designs included Von Ferbulis (Austria and Washington, DC); McGinnis, Walsh & Sullivan (Boston); J. De Mentureal (Paris); Rudell & Odenthal (Cologne), architects for Holy Cross Church (8115 Church Road, St. Louis); and Barnett, Haynes & Barnett, the only local firm to enter.

After Archbishop Glennon toured European cathedrals in late summer 1905, he stated the new St. Louis cathedral should combine Romanesque, Byzantine, and Renaissance styles. He felt strongly about the style of the architecture, saying, "Gothic architecture, with its pointed arches and spires, reaches toward heaven. But Byzantine architecture, with its splendid domes, brings heaven down to earth."

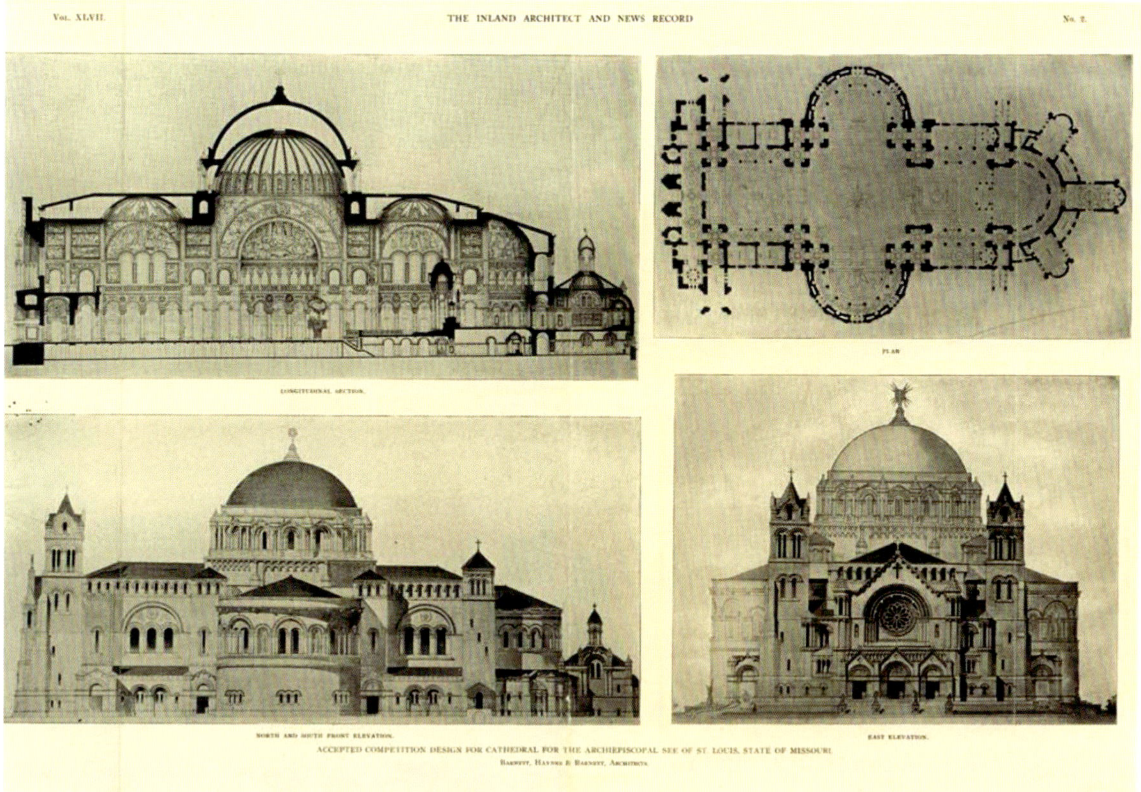

St. Louis Cathedral

Four views. Accepted design for the cathedral for the Archepiscopal See of St. Louis. Consecrated 1926, interior fully finished in 1988

Cathedral Basilica of Saint Louis, 4431 Lindell Blvd., St. Louis, Missouri. Barnett, Haynes & Barnett, architects. From *Inland Architect*, vol. 47, no. 2. Courtesy of Ryerson and Burnham Art and Architecture Archives, The Art Institute of Chicago

1906: A Winner

The stated goals of the design competition were for a structure of $1 million that would not be classic, Gothic, or Renaissance in style.

In order to review the comparative merits of all the plans submitted, a committee of three architectural experts was employed to assist in the selection of the plan, which would give the best and most artistic development of the proposed design as set forth in the code of the competition.

On February 12, 1906, after a long session with several spirited discussions while reviewing the cathedral competition entries, the special committee rendered its verdict in favor of the design by Barnett, Haynes & Barnett.

George Dennis Barnett (1863–1922) designed a Byzantine interior within a Romanesque exterior structure. Without copying any church in the world, he created a new combination of ancient Romanesque and Byzantine styles for the Cathedral of Saint Louis.

On September 2, 1906, it was announced that work would commence as soon as the architects had prepared the drawings. Archbishop Glennon remarked: "We hope to have a very large and beautiful structure. Its seating capacity is estimated at between 4,000 and 5,000, and its cost will be at least $1 million. We do not expect to go into debt. It is a bad thing to have a mortgage between you and the Almighty."

New Cathedral east elevation postcard. Courtesy of Archdiocese of St. Louis Archives

1906: Refining the Design

With their selection in the design competition, the architects immediately began to prepare the detailed drawings for construction of the New Cathedral of St. Louis, featuring a Byzantine interior within a Romanesque exterior structure.

Barnett compared the dimensions of length, width, and height, as well as areas and seating capacities of the New Cathedral, with Westminster Cathedral of London, England, with the New Cathedral greater in every way.

Gray granite with a fine texture was selected from quarries in Concord, New Hampshire. It lent itself to elaborate carvings, sculptured and decorated motifs.

The central dome covered in green-glazed roof tile surmounted by a granite lunette with gold cross was intended to attract the eye from any part of the city.

The magnificent interiors of dramatic scale and domes, rich materials of marbles and mosaics, were intended to provide an ever-changing vista of design.

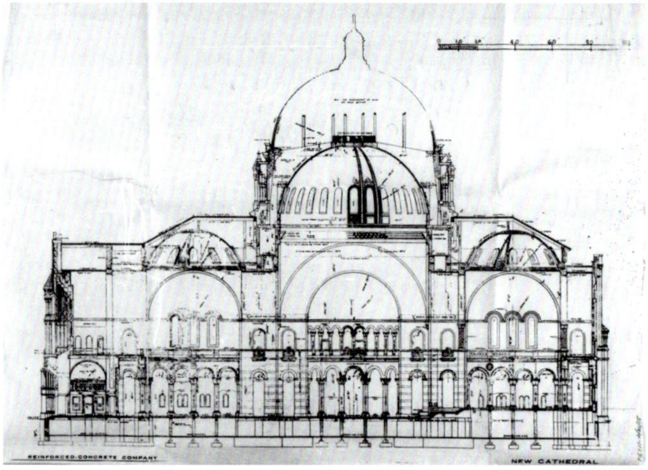

New Cathedral longitudinal section

Courtesy of Archdiocese of St. Louis Building and Real Estate Archives

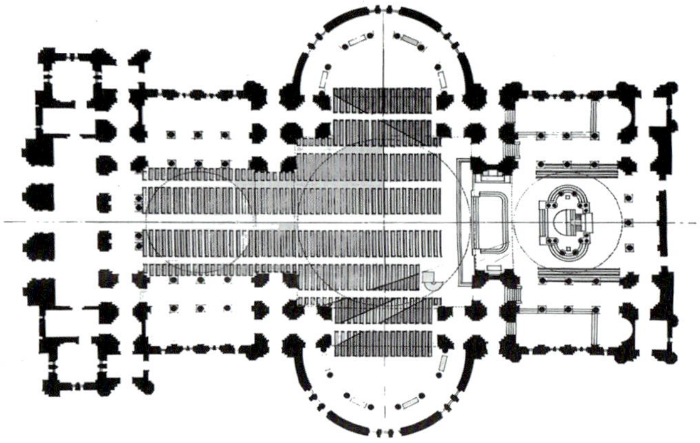

New Cathedral floor plan

Courtesy of Cathedral Basilica of Saint Louis Archives

1906: A New Site?

After evaluating various options, Archbishop John J. Kain purchased the cathedral lot property in 1895 on Lindell Boulevard and Newstead Avenue. Most people thought this location was the most suitable for the New Cathedral. In 1906, Barnett, Haynes & Barnett prepared the construction documents.

Still, in the minds of some, doubts lingered if this site was the most satisfactory. It was claimed that Archbishop Glennon favored abandoning this site and hoped to build farther west. Indeed, on December 2, 1906, the *St. Louis Republic* reported that "the plans for the edifice are nearly complete and the architects are soon to ask for bids for construction." It went on to report, "It is stated on good authority, however, that the Most Reverend Archbishop John J. Glennon hopes to build the Cathedral on a site farther west and is strongly in favor of the abandonment of the site originally selected. In this he is said to have the support of his consultors. The site favored by the Archbishop has not been made public by him or his council."

While this alternative site remains a mystery, one cannot help but wonder if it might have

New Cathedral east elevation. Courtesy of Cathedral Basilica of Saint Louis Archives

been at Kingshighway Boulevard and Lindell Boulevard—the entire block of eight acres, from Lindell Boulevard to Maryland Avenue and Kingshighway to Euclid Avenue—owned by William K. Bixby (1857–1931), businessman and philanthropist, president of American Car and Foundry, president of Washington University and the Art Museum of St. Louis, and a trustee of the St. Louis Public Library. He was a collector of art, rare books, and artifacts, and a cultural benefactor to St. Louis. This block was previously owned by John W. Kauffman (1844–1904), a flour company magnate, grain dealer and speculator, owner of the Kauffman Milling Company, and president of the Merchants' Exchange of St. Louis, who built a 45-room mansion with an art gallery, greenhouses, and stables on the property.

This magnificent property overlooked the site of the 1904 World's Fair and would have been in keeping with the westward movement of religious institutions in St. Louis, such as the Holy Corners (1902) on North Kingshighway Boulevard between and including Westminster Place and Washington Avenue.

Plans Nearly Completed for New St. Louis Cathedral and Contract for Construction Will Soon Be Let

THE CATHEDRAL AS IT WILL APPEAR, ACCORDING TO LATEST DESIGN.

"Plans Nearly Completed for New St. Louis Cathedral and Contract for Construction Will Soon Be Let." *St. Louis Republic*, December 2, 1906
Courtesy of St. Louis Public Library–Central Library

1907–14: May 1, 1907, Groundbreaking

Given the importance of confirming the site for the New Cathedral, a committee was appointed to study the question and canvass the various sections of the West End for a more suitable location. Early in February 1907, at a meeting of the members of the Cathedral Board and several large subscribers to the fund, the committee reported in favor of the site on Lindell Boulevard and Newstead Avenue. With unanimous approval to proceed with this site, a few days later the soil was tested, with rock found approximately 15 feet below the surface. Examination proved the ground could safely support the tremendous weight of the Cathedral of Saint Louis.

Ground was broken on May 1, 1907, with Archbishop Glennon raising the first spadeful of earth, thus inaugurating the work. Also present were Archbishop Jeremiah Harty of Manila—the first native-born St. Louisan to become a bishop; Reverend Francis Gilfillan, rector of the Cathedral Chapel; Reverend J. J. Tannrath of the Chancery office, the pastor; and George D. Barnett of Barnett, Haynes & Barnett, architects of the cathedral, who measured the building footprint and marked the exact center.

Reverend P. H. Bradley, entrusted with the building supervision; John Haynes, architect; and Jerome F. P. Casey, builder of the foundations, also participated in the groundbreaking. Archbishop Glennon said, "Mr. Casey shall be the last, and then we will leave him to do the rest of the digging."

George D. Barnett explained to those gathered that the grade of the site was to be raised to the level of Taylor Avenue, resulting in the main floor being 8 feet above Lindell Boulevard. The cathedral walls would be set back 60 feet from Lindell Boulevard and 75 feet from Newstead Avenue.

The excavation began at once!

GROUND IS BROKEN FOR NEW CATHOLIC CATHEDRAL; ARCHBISHOP GLENNON RAISES THE FIRST SPADEFUL

From left to right: Rev. Francis Gilfillan, rector of cathedral chapel; Archbishop Harty of Manila, Archbishop Glennon, Rev. J. J. Tannrath, George D. Barnett, architect of the cathedral.

Standing in the center of the cathedral site, where in time to come the lofty dome will rise 240 feet, Archbishop Glennon raised the first spadeful of earth yesterday to inaugurate the actual work of building the cathedral. Architect George D. Barnett of Barnett, Haynes & Barnett, measured off the space and marked what would be the exact center.

Archbishop Harty of Manila was Archbishop Glennon's guest and assisted with the second spadeful. Rev. Francis Gilfillan, rector of the cathedral chapel; Rev. J. J. Tannrath of the chancery office and Rev. P. H. Bradley, to whom the building supervision is intrusted, all lent a hand in the undertaking. Mr. Barnett lifted a spadeful and John Hynes, who is moving the parochial residence, took part. Last came Jerome F. P. Casey, builder of the foundations.

"Mr. Casey shall be last," said Archbishop Glennon, "and then we will leave him to do the rest of the digging."

The occasion was quite informal. Mr. Barnett explained on the ground some of the particulars of the architect's plans. The grade is to be raised to the level of Taylor avenue, which will make the floor about 8 feet above the ground. The cathedral walls will stand 60 feet back from Lindell avenue and 75 feet back from Newstead avenue.

Moving Parochial Residence.

The archbishop and the priests stayed to witness the start of the moving of the parochial residence. For thirty-five days preparations for this have been going on. It is an unusually large house to move, and it has been placed on 8-inch rollers, seven sets of six rollers each on each side of the house, with a similar set of seven times six rollers through the central portion. Props and braces, cables and levers, were all nicely adjusted, and the team of horses at a distant winding-post stood ready for the archbishop to witness the start. A wheezing and a heaving sounded, and the house groaned and began its journey, muslin curtains quivereing in the breeze, and tinware chattering in the kitchen.

The house moved 4 inches, then it stopped suddenly. A chain had snapped. This had to be repaired, and no more moving was done at that time, but it is to proceed to-day, and will soon be accomplished. The house is ultimately to stand facing Maryland avenue, to the west of the cathedral chapel, leaving the central space clear for the cathedral. Rumor says that in time a residence for the archbishop may be added to the cathedral building.

Groundbreaking for the Cathedral of Saint Louis

St. Louis Globe-Democrat, May 2, 1907

Courtesy of Archdiocese of St. Louis Archives

1907–14: Foundations

Construction occurred over seven years, between 1907 and 1914, commencing on May 1, 1907. Foundations were built with remarkable speed and thoroughness by the St. Louis Contracting Company (Jerome P. F. Casey, vice president), which employed 420 men on-site. Of note, the St. Louis Contracting Company, commonly known as Casey & O'Toole, was founded in 1892 by cousins Jerome Casey and George O'Toole. George's father, Timothy J. O'Toole (1844–1921), was an Irish immigrant who helped build the stone piers of the Eads Bridge (1867–74).

Hannick Quarry & Construction Company supplied the stone from a quarry at North Euclid and Ashland Avenue, now W. C. Handy Park.

Plans for the entire superstructure were finally completed and submitted by the architects. The drawings were on exhibition at the archiepiscopal residence, 3810 Lindell Boulevard, on New Year's Day, and immediately distributed to the prospective contractors.

After additional discussions about the type of stone to be used, granite or Bedford stone, on April 9, 1908, a committee of five recommended the use of granite, which was then unanimously approved by the Board. This decision raised the cost of the structure by $300,000.

The contract for the superstructure for the cathedral amounting to $1 million was awarded to J. C. Robinson & Son of New York on May 10, 1908.

New Cathedral, construction of foundation

Courtesy of Archdiocese of St. Louis Archives

Temporary Cathedral Chapel, Newstead Ave. and Maryland Ave., with foundation construction underway in 1907

Courtesy of Archdiocese of St. Louis Archives

New Cathedral, construction of foundation, Hannick Quarry & Construction Company

Courtesy of Archdiocese of St. Louis Archives

1907–14: Superstructure

Planning, architectural and structural design, and the construction documents for the Cathedral of Saint Louis were prepared by Barnett, Haynes & Barnett, architects; the Reinforced-Concrete Company, structural concrete engineers; and Brussel & Viterbo, consulting engineers. J. C. Robinson & Son, building contactors, were awarded the contract to build this magnificent structure.

The construction of the Cathedral of Saint Louis began on May 1, 1907. Three crane towers to hoist materials were strategically located and erected. In December of 1908, the "concreters" placed the concrete, reinforced with steel, for the first floor, supported by the basement walls.

New Cathedral crane towers, ca.1910. A. Leschen & Sons Rope Co. pamphlet, ca. 1910

Courtesy of Archdiocese of St. Louis Archives

The concreters laying the first floor, December 12, 1908

From *Notable Catholic Institutions* (1911)

Courtesy of St. Louis Public Library–Central Library

Cornerstone of the New Cathedral

From *The Great St. Louis Cathedral*, by William B. Faherty, SJ (1988)

Courtesy of Archdiocese of St. Louis Archives

Blessing of cornerstone of the Cathedral of Saint Louis

From *The Great St. Louis Cathedral* by William B. Faherty, SJ

Courtesy of Archdiocese of St. Louis Archives

Laying of the cornerstone of the New Cathedral on October 18, 1908

Courtesy of Archdiocese of St. Louis Archives

1907–14: October 18, 1908, Cornerstone

On October 18, 1908, the laying of the cornerstone began with an impressive parade of 40,000 members of 79 parishes marching to the cathedral site westward on Lindell Boulevard from Grand Avenue, passing under an archway made of intertwined Papal and American flags.

For 2 hours and 10 minutes they passed by the reviewing stand filled with numerous Church dignitaries, including the Apostolic Delegate, Archbishop Diomede Falconio, who blessed the cornerstone, along with Bishop John M. Farley of New York, Archbishop John Ireland of St. Paul, and Archbishop Glennon, who gave a moving address to close the ceremony.

The cornerstone was set in the southeast corner of the cathedral. Within a hollowed receptacle in the stone were deposited a collection of valuable coins, including some of every nation; copies of the St. Louis newspapers; the parchment scroll, written in Latin, attesting the events of the day; and photographs of Bishop Rosati, His Excellency the Apostolic Delegate, Cardinal Gibbons, Pope Pius X, and Archbishops Kenrick, Ryan, Kain, and Glennon.

The Latin inscription on the cornerstone, made of Missouri granite reads, translated: “To Christ triumphant, and in honor of St. Louis, King of France, patron of this dear city and Archdiocese, this cornerstone of the Metropolitan Church to be erected through the generosity of the whole Archdiocese was laid on the 18th day of October, 1908, by His Excellency the Delegate of the Apostolic See.”

1907–14: Steel and Stone

By May of 1909, granite stone was being hoisted into place for the west front tower. Iron workers erected the steel floor beams while other iron workers used hand forges to heat rivets to connect the columns and beams. Bricklayers built the pier walls. By early July 1909, the granite walls forming the three main arched entrances were being erected.

Iron workers are putting in the steel floor beams while bricklayers are working on the piers, May 1, 1909

From *Notable Catholic Institutions* (1911). Courtesy of St. Louis Public Library–Central Library

The iron workers using the hand forge to heat rivets

From *Notable Catholic Institutions* (1911). Courtesy of St. Louis Public Library–Central Library

The derricks showing one of the "skips" for hoisting brick and cement, July 3, 1909. View showing one of the three main entrance doorways in the course of construction. From *Notable Catholic Institutions* (1911). Courtesy of St. Louis Public Library–Central Library

1907–14: Shaping the Stone

Later in July 1909, the granite walls were installed on the gallery or clerestory level. Stonecutters worked adjacent to the St. Louis Cathedral Chapel, just to the north of the cathedral construction, shaping the granite stones for the walls and capitals.

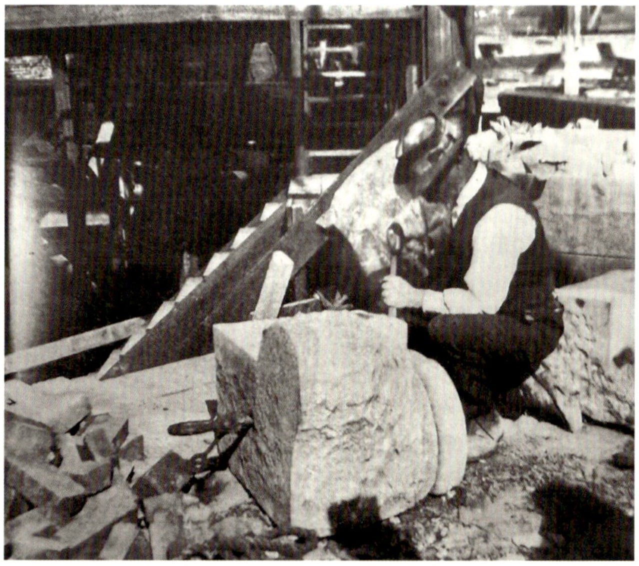

The stone cutters recutting a column cap
From *Notable Catholic Institutions* (1911)
Courtesy of St. Louis Public Library–Central Library

Laying the granite, July 23, 1909
From *Notable Catholic Institutions* (1911)
Courtesy of St. Louis Public Library–Central Library

The stone cutters working adjacent to the Cathedral Chapel
From *Notable Catholic Institutions* (1911). Courtesy of St. Louis Public Library– Central Library

1907–14: Forms in Concrete

As construction progressed, the builders worked at great heights. Carpenters erected scaffolding, creating platforms for the concreters to stand on while hoisting the hoppers to pour the concrete into the formwork.

Plumbers installed internal downspouts in the walls to inconspicuously drain the water from the roofs.

The concreters hoisting and dumping into the hopper and pouring the concrete

From *Notable Catholic Institutions* (1911). Courtesy of St. Louis Public Library–Central Library

1907–14: Bricklayers and Stone Setters

The bricklayers and the stone setters worked side by side as they built the west transept of the cathedral. The bricklayers formed wood arches in order to construct the masonry arches called for by the design of the Romanesque exterior. The bricklayers also built the piers that helped support the main dome.

The bricklayers with centers of the forming arches set with bricklayers putting in the brick. From *Notable Catholic Institutions* (1911). Courtesy of St. Louis Public Library–Central Library

The stone setters at work

Courtesy of Arteaga Photos LTD.

The bricklayers constructing the great temple

From *Notable Catholic Institutions* (1911)

Courtesy of St. Louis Public Library–Central Library

1907–14: A Modern Structure for Traditional Forms

The structural design for the Cathedral of Saint Louis was prepared by the Reinforced-Concrete Company, structural concrete engineers, and Brussel & Viterbo, consulting engineers.

The bricklayers and the stone setters built the semicircular east and west transepts of the cathedral, thus forming the Celtic cruciform plan with the main sanctuary, as the walls rose up around the three great crane towers within the volume.

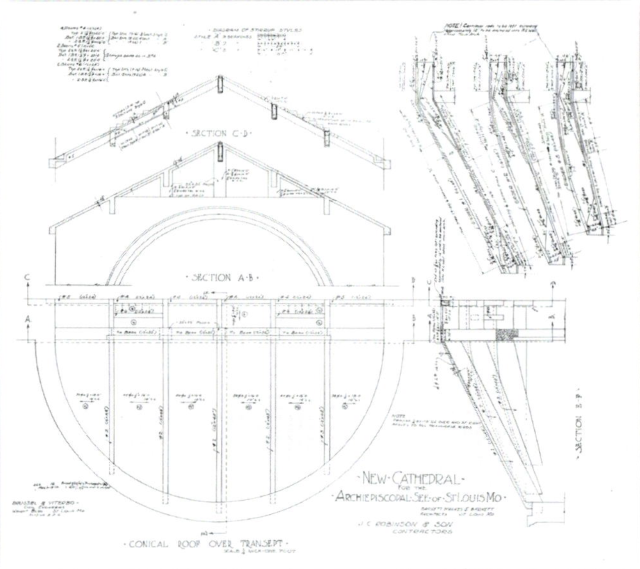

Conical roof over transept

From *Structural Reinforced-Concrete in the New Cathedral* (1911)

Courtesy of Archdiocese of St. Louis Archives

The bricklayers and the stone setters–the west transept of the cathedral in process of construction

From *Notable Catholic Institutions* (1911). Courtesy of St. Louis Public Library–Central Library

The walls of the Cathedral of Saint Louis rise up, ca. 1909

From *Notable Catholic Institutions* (1911). Courtesy of St. Louis Public Library–Central Library

1907–14:
Rising to New Heights

The walls of the cathedral continued to rise to greater heights with three crane towers strategically positioned for the derricks to lift materials to builders above.

Archbishop Glennon on tour of inspection of the Cathedral

From *Notable Catholic Institutions* (1911). Courtesy of St. Louis Public Library–Central Library

The laborers loading the buckets with materials for the builders

From *Notable Catholic Institutions* (1911). Courtesy of St. Louis Public Library–Central Library

The walls of the Cathedral of Saint Louis rise up, ca. 1909

From *Notable Catholic Institutions* (1911). Courtesy of St. Louis Public Library–Central Library

1907–14: Reinforced to Last

Reinforced concrete was used for its great strength and longevity, making the cathedral structure, with its large spans and striking forms, both modern and fireproof.

Reinforced concrete wind bracing of main outside dome, September 20, 1910

From *Structural Reinforced-Concrete in the New Cathedral* (1911)

Courtesy of Archdiocese of St. Louis Archives

Reinforcement of girder supporting main dome across corners

From *Structural Reinforced-Concrete in the New Cathedral* (1911)

Courtesy of Archdiocese of St. Louis Archives

The "signal man" whose duties are to give the signal for the hoisting of materials

From *Notable Catholic Institutions* (1911). Courtesy of St. Louis Public Library–Central Library

1907–14: A Modern Inner Structure

George D. Barnett noted, "The materials throughout are absolutely fireproof and of most modern development. All structural features are of reinforced concrete in which new and original structural formations have been employed and are attracting the attention of the architects and engineers of the world, taking interest in this structural phase as modernly applied." The magnificent central dome, as well as the overall cathedral, stand in testimony to this statement.

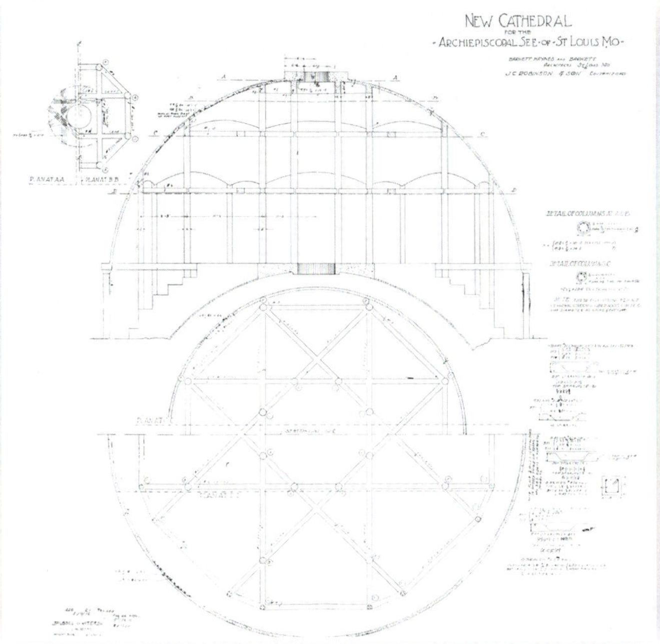

Structural frame of main dome
From *Structural Reinforced-Concrete in the New Cathedral* (1911)
Courtesy of Archdiocese of St. Louis Archives

Reinforced concrete wind bracing of main outside dome
From *Structural Reinforced-Concrete in the New Cathedral* (1911)
Courtesy of Archdiocese of St. Louis Archives

Compression ring at crown of main inside dome
From *Structural Reinforced-Concrete in the New Cathedral* (1911)
Courtesy of Archdiocese of St. Louis Archives

1907–14: Magnificent Volumes

The interior volumes of the New Cathedral, grand and majestic in scale, with a Byzantine architectural composition of great dimensions, were revealed during the construction of the impressive reinforced concrete structure.

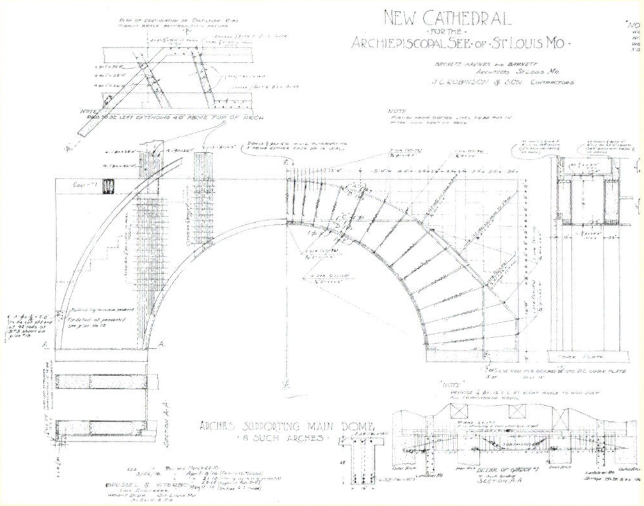

Arches supporting main dome

From *Structural Reinforced-Concrete in the New Cathedral* (1911)
Courtesy of Archdiocese of St. Louis Archives

Exterior construction, 1911. *Electric St. Louis Magazine*, August 1911
Courtesy of Archdiocese of St. Louis Archives

Interior before installation of mosaics, 1911. From *Structural Reinforced Concrete in the New Cathedral* (1911)

Courtesy of Archdiocese of St. Louis Archives

1907–14: The Team

In writing of the contractors for the Cathedral of St. Louis, George D. Barnett expressed his admiration and gratitude as follows: "To Whose Untiring Energy and Skill in Faithfully, Intelligently and Honestly Carrying Out the Plans for the Building of the Cathedral, St. Louis will Owe another Debt of Gratitude."

The architects of the cathedral

Barnett, Haynes & Barnett, architects

From *Notable Catholic Institutions* (1911)
Courtesy of St. Louis Public Library–Central Library

The contractors of the cathedral

J.C. Robinson & Son, Building Contactors

From *Notable Catholic Institutions* (1911)
Courtesy of St. Louis Public Library–Central Library

George D. Barnett

Tom P. Barnett

John I. Haynes

John C. Robinson

Roy H. Robinson

The superintendents and foremen included Henry Bell, building foreman; Hymers Austin, yard foreman; N. J. Casey, plumbers' foreman; F. W. Hagloch, superintendent of construction; O. W. Krum, quarry manager; George D. Barnett, head architect; Andrew Gray, granite setting foreman; H. G. Goodwin, general manager; Joe DeBano, derrick foreman; H. O. Clarke, carpenter foreman; O. F. Haggerty, labor foreman; and John Cerink, contractors' engineer.

From *Notable Catholic Institutions* (1911). Courtesy of St. Louis Public Library–Central Library

Key members of the management and construction group

From *Notable Catholic Institutions* (1911). Courtesy of St. Louis Public Library–Central Library

The Cathedral of Saint Louis seen in context, August 20, 1913
Photograph "compliments of the architects," Barnett, Haynes & Barnett
Courtesy of Archdiocese of St. Louis Archives

Interior view looking northwest
From *Structural Reinforced Concrete in the New Cathedral* (1911). Courtesy of Archdiocese of St. Louis Archives

An Alexander and Sons Mortuary spokesman described this photo as showing the first all-motorized funeral in St. Louis in October 1911 at the Cathedral of Saint Louis, which was still under construction at the time.

St. Louis Review/Christian Burial Supplement, October 31,1980

Courtesy of Cathedral Basilica of Saint Louis Archives

1907–14: A Dominant Profile

As the superstructure drew near completion in 1914, the architects had a photograph made of their magnificent design from an elevated point of view and gave it to Archbishop John J. Glennon, with "compliments of the architects," inscribed on the back side of the photograph.

As George D. Barnett, architect, wrote in 1911, "The central or dome feature will be strongly marked with its pedimented and pylon bays, surmounted by a granite lunette with gold cross, which will, by its great height, attract the eye from any part of the city.

"Two campaniles will flank either side of the facade.

"The roofs will all be covered with [a specially] made green glazed tile and decoration, glinting in the sunlight, forming a pleasing color combination with the granite materials."

1907–14: The Mother Church

After seven years of construction, the Cathedral Basilica superstructure was completed in 1914. Its massive proportions were something to behold.

It was 350 feet north to south and 204 feet east to west overall. The central dome soared to 217 feet, while the twin towers were 157 feet above street level. The floor space totaled 44,460 square feet.

The Cathedral of Saint Louis—the Mother Church of St. Louis—reflects the generation that built it, as they drew from the ancient architectural traditions of the Romanesque and Byzantine to identify with iconic Old World structures, while adapting them to meet the needs of their time.

The Cathedral of Saint Louis rises up majestically from the surrounding neighborhood, serving those who live in the residences, apartments, and hotels nearby.

The Mother Church
Courtesy of The State Historical Society of Missouri

Postcard with Cathedral Chapel to the north, ca. 1914
Courtesy of The State Historical Society of Missouri

October 18, 1914: First Mass

Six years to the day after the laying of the cornerstone, the first Mass was celebrated on Sunday October 18, 1914, by Bishop John J. Hennessy, former pastor of St. John's Pro-Cathedral in St. Louis, and now the first bishop of Wichita, Kansas (1889).

The Cathedral of Saint Louis was solemnly blessed on this beautiful early autumn day, with a magnificent crowd of worshippers of every creed, race, and social strata gathered for the Pontifical Mass. The archbishop was joined by ecclesiastics and seminarians in a procession of blessing around the walls of the cathedral. Those gathered sang a hymn of praise, along with a choir of 300, filling the half-finished interiors of the cathedral and its chapels.

Archbishop John J. Glennon sat on the archiepiscopal throne, flanked by his two chaplains, along with more than 30 priests in the sanctuary. Before the sermon proper, the archbishop spoke about the finances, including receipts of $1,729,648 and expenditures amounting to $1,302,000, noting, "We opened without debt and we have funds on hand for every contract thus far signed."

Given the unfinished decorations and equipment, the solemn consecration would wait until a later date. Of note, the south rose window of deep-blue glass by Tiffany Company of New York was installed before the New Cathedral dedication on October 18, 1914. The north rose window of red glass was installed shortly thereafter. Both rose windows were donated by Mr. and Mrs. William J. Kinsella.

Archbishop Glennon went on to explain the significance of the cathedral, contrasting the Byzantine style of the Cathedral of Saint Louis with the Gothic architecture of many European cathedrals. "The Gothic spire, like a prayer offered, goes upward to the skies; the Byzantine, like unto a prayer answered, brings the dome of heaven down to earth. One is a prayer asked, the other a prayer answered."

The south rose window features glass of deep color values developed and made by the Tiffany Company of New York.

Photograph by Serhii Chrucky © Serhii Chrucky I Esto

New St. Louis Cathedral from street level

Photographer Oscar C. Kuehn. September 16, 1916

Courtesy of Missouri Historical Society

Wedding of Kathleen McBride and Lacy Marion Love, Cathedral of Saint Louis, October 20, 1914
Courtesy of Cathedral Basilica of Saint Louis Museum

October 20, 1914: First Wedding

The first wedding in the Cathedral of Saint Louis, that of Kathleen McBride, daughter of the donors of the high altar—William Cullen McBride (1859–1917) and his wife, Katherine Manan McBride—and Lacy Marion Love, was witnessed by Archbishop Glennon on October 20, 1914. The High Mass was sung by Pastor Francis Gilfillan.

With the interior of the cathedral unfinished, more than $3,000 in lavish decorations were brought in to transform the dramatic volume. Twenty blossoming orange trees were brought to St. Louis from California in heated cars. More than 5,000 white chrysanthemums and 50 cases of smilax, covering the walls from the balcony promenade to the floor, dominated the floral arrangement, which also included orchids, ferns, and 700 palms. Four large urns, filled with 200 chrysanthemums, were placed near the altar. Twenty prie-dieu at the altar were trimmed with white satin, each with a nosegay of orange blossoms. White satin rope and house decorations completed the setting.

The decorations were under the supervision of Grimm & Gorly, florists. Henri Dueroberg, designer for the floral company, was in charge of the decorations. Twenty-five men worked 52 hours to decorate the new Cathedral of Saint Louis before the noon wedding.

Kathleen McBride was accompanied by seven bridesmaids.

William Cullen McBride, born on January 13, 1859, in Butler, Pennsylvania, moved to St. Louis, Missouri, in 1908 with his wife and their four daughters (Ellen, Laura, Kathleen, and Dorothy). They lived at 29 Washington Terrace. He became the largest independent oil producer in the United States, with an estate valued at more than $10 million at the time of his death in 1917 at 58 years old.

1915: First Mosaics

On July 2, 1912, the contracts for the Chapel of Our Lady and the All Saints Chapel were awarded to the Tiffany Company of New York. The plans and drawings for these chapels were prepared by the Italian architect Aristide Leonori in the Italian style, which uses colored marble tesserae with a more limited choice of color, is duller, and lacks the reflective quality of Byzantine-style reflective colored glass tesserae and gold leaf tesserae. He supervised the design of the layout drawings, referred to as cartoons, and the assembling of the marbles and mosaics.

The mosaics in the Chapel of Our Lady portray Mary's Presentation, Annunciation, Visitation to Elizabeth, and the Assumption. The mosaics of the All Saints Chapel portray the early classification of saints as either Apostles, confessors, martyrs, or virgins.

In 1913, a vast decorative scheme for the cathedral showing symbolic ornamentation in mosaics, marbles, and precious metals was prepared by Aristides Leonori & Company, classical architects, Rome, and was illustrated in the *St. Louis Post-Dispatch Sunday Magazine* on May 18.

On March 7, 1914, the *American Art News* reported that the mosaics for the two chapels were on exhibition at the Tiffany Studios of New York, featuring the dome and series of triptychs surmounted by lunettes, all framed in white marble. The scenes portrayed the life of the Virgin and the Patron Saints of the Church.

The two chapels were completed in the summer of 1915. Archbishop Glennon celebrated the first Mass in the All Saints Chapel on October 10, 1915, which was offered for the eternal repose of the soul of the donor of the chapel, Mrs. Anne Hamilton Bailey.

The All Saints Chapel is south of the west transept, and the gift of Anna Hamilton Bailey.

Photographs by John C. Guenther, FAIA, LEED AP

The Chapel of Our Lady is north of the west transept, and is the gift of the Sheehan-Lamy Family.

1915: The Kilgen Chancel Organ

The Kilgen chancel organ, gift of James W. Garneau (1858–1922) and the Garneau family of St. Louis, was blessed by Archbishop Glennon on August 25, 1915, the Feast of Saint Louis, after the solemn Mass in honor of the patron saint of the city. By a sad coincidence, that very same week, the $10,000 organ donated by the Garneau family accompanied the funeral Mass for John B. Garneau (1871–1915).

The organ had two duplicate four-manual consoles, one placed in the gallery with the main organ and the other in the sanctuary behind the main altar with a smaller instrument. There was also a celestial division whose pipes were in the dome of the cathedral.

The George Kilgen and Son church and parlor pipe organs company was established in New York in 1851 and in St. Louis in 1873.

In the same year of 1915, the new Kenrick Theological Seminary opened its doors to faculty and students, after the former Kenrick Seminary, located on Cass Avenue and 19th Street, had become inadequate. Archbishop Glennon bought part of the old Benton (Drummond) Farm, later renamed Glennon Park, south of Shrewsbury.

The new Kenrick Seminary was designed by Comès & Imbs, architects, for the formation of priests. The plan was organized with philosophy in the east wing, the chapel in the central wing, and theology in the west wing.

Ground was broken on April 28, 1913. The cornerstone was laid on November 27, 1913—Thanksgiving Day. The faculty and students took possession of the Seminary on September 13–15, 1915. Archbishop Glennon formally dedicated the new Kenrick Seminary on April 27, 1916.

The Kilgen Chancel organ
Gift of the Garneau family of St. Louis (1915)
Courtesy of Cathedral Basilica of Saint Louis Archives

Kenrick Theological Seminary (1913–15). Comès & Imbs, architects
Courtesy of Archdiocese of Saint Louis Archives

William Theodore Diebels was the New Cathedral's first organist-choirmaster from 1915 to 1940. He is pictured with his boys' choirs, playing the front console. There was also a four-manual console in the gallery, and pipes throughout the cathedral.

Courtesy of Cathedral Basilica of Saint Louis Museum

High altar and baldacchino

From *Art World*, vol. 2, no. 3, June 1917

Cathedral School, 1916

Courtesy of Archdiocese of St. Louis Archives

Aerial view of Cathedral of Saint Louis and Cathedral School

Courtesy of Archdiocese of St. Louis Archives

1916: The Baldacchino

George D. Barnett designed the high altar, the baldacchino, the Calvary scene, and the mosaics within the interior and exterior of the baldacchino's dome, as well as the mosaics on the three sides of the sanctuary's arched lower walls. The $100,000 project was funded by William Cullen McBride and his wife, Katherine Manan McBride

On November 17, 1913, the Gorham Company of New York City and Providence, Rhode Island, was commissioned to build the high altar according to the plans and specifications submitted by Barnett. Two years of fabrication and installation followed, with the Gorham Company working with craftsmen in Italy. The Byzantine mosaics of the interior and exterior of the baldacchino dome, as well as the three sides of the sanctuary's lower arcade walls, were designed by Barnett and were completed in October of 1916.

On November 2, 1916, the high altar was inaugurated by Archbishop Glennon, who presided at the first Solemn Pontifical Mass on the Feast of All Souls and offered the Mass for the deceased benefactors of the cathedral.

With the mosaic designs by Barnett of the baldacchino and surrounding walls, a significant stylistic break was realized from the mosaics by Tiffany in the All Saints and Our Lady's Chapels.

The central dome and two semicircular transepts repeat the structural forms of the cathedral's central dome and transepts, and thus are a church within a church, 57 feet in height with a diameter of 36 feet. The dome is supported by 14 columns carved from Italian marbles of various colors.

The Cathedral School opened in 1916 to the west of the Cathedral of Saint Louis.

1917: The Blessed Sacrament Chapel

George D. Barnett of Barnett, Haynes & Barnett—architects of the entire Cathedral of Saint Louis—designed the Blessed Sacrament Chapel and the adjacent red-ceilinged ambulatory, to the west of the sanctuary.

The Blessed Sacrament Chapel mosaics were fabricated and installed by the Gorham Company of New York and Rhode Island and are the most Byzantine of any of the four side chapels. The dominant color is red, which is symbolic of the saving Blood of Christ. The special red pigment for the mosaics was created just for tiles in the church's Blessed Sacrament side chapel and its hallway. The pigment was destroyed so the color recipe could not be copied elsewhere.

The Blessed Sacrament Chapel was completed in March of 1917 but not used until Holy Thursday, April 5, 1917, when Monsignor Francis Gilfillan celebrated Mass there. The chapel was a gift of the late Honorable Richard C. Kerens, an ambassador to Austria, in memory of his deceased wife.

The south entrance to the Blessed Sacrament Chapel features two elaborate bronze gates, originally part of the Austrian Exhibit at the 1904 Louisiana Purchase Exhibition in St. Louis, and donated by the Austrian government to Archbishop Glennon.

Ironically, the Blessed Sacrament Chapel was completed in March of 1917, three days before Austria and the United States cut diplomatic ties before World War I.

With the United States entering into World War I in April 1917, further work was stopped as the nation dedicated its resources to the war effort. The United States Senate, in a 74 to 0 vote, declared war on Austria-Hungary on December 7, 1917.

Ambulatory west of the Blessed Sacrament Chapel

Photograph by John C. Guenther, FAIA, LEED AP

South entrance to the Blessed Sacrament Chapel with bronze gates from Austrian Exhibit

Photograph by Serhii Chrucky © Serhii Chrucky I Esto

Mosaic for bishop's throne (1920)
Courtesy of Cathedral Basilica of Saint Louis Archives

Emil Frei, Sr. (third from left) with studio artists, ca. 1912
Courtesy of Emil Frei & Associates, Inc.

Glass mosaics for ornate stone pulpit (1921)
Photographs by Serhii Chrucky © Serhii Chrucky I Esto

1920–21: Emil Frei Art Glass Company

With the Chapel of Our Lady and All Saints Chapel mosaics designed and installed by the Tiffany Studios and the high altar and baldacchino fabricated by the Gorham Company, along with the Blessed Sacrament Chapel and adjacent ambulatory, and with a pause in construction due to World War I, Archbishop Glennon considered local companies to proceed with the Byzantine-style mosaics he envisioned.

Emil Frei, Sr. (1869–1942) was born in Zöschlingsweiler in Bavaria. He studied at the School of Fine Arts in Munich and worked as a muralist in Bavaria before emigrating in 1894. Arriving in St. Louis, he painted art glass for residences for the A.H. Wallis Company.

In 1898, Emil Frei, Sr. founded the Emil Frei Art Glass Company, which grew rapidly with its artists and craftsmen fabricating stained glass for St. Francis de Sales and St. Anthony of Padua churches in St. Louis, and for other churches across the country.

Of note, Emil Frei Art Glass Company had won the grand prize at the Louisiana Purchase Exhibition in 1904 for stained glass windows commissioned for Holy Family Church in Watertown, New York.

Emil Frei Art Glass had worked in mosaics prior to 1909. The grand scale of the Cathedral of Saint Louis and its anticipated Byzantine mosaic projects offered an opportunity for the company to expand its mosaic work.

The first mosaic commissions for the cathedral by Emil Frei Art Glass began in 1920 with three projects, including inlaid mosaics for the bishop's throne in the sanctuary and in the ornate stone pulpit.

The pulpit was the gift of the Very Reverend Francis Gilfillan, rector of the cathedral from 1907 to 1922.

1922: Rosati-Kain High School

In 1911, the School Sisters of Notre Dame and the Sisters of St. Joseph of Carondelet opened the Rosati Center and the Kain School. The two schools merged to create Rosati-Kain High School and moved into the St. Vincent site on Grand and Lucas.

In 1919, the school moved to the Hayes Mansion on Lindell and Newstead. In 1921, the Hayes Mansion was moved to the northwest corner of the lot facing Newstead.

By September 1922, the three-story classical structure, designed by architect Henry P. Hess, was completed. Funds for the construction of the building were donated by Archbishop Glennon from money received as gifts on the occasion of his Silver Episcopal Jubilee.

Between 1917 and 1921, George D. Barnett continued his mosaic designs for the transepts of the New Cathedral with its two levels of arcades, providing concepts for the Byzantine mosaic decoration of the arches above the columns.

Sadly, Barnett developed a severe case of pneumonia, which kept him from actively working during his last year of life, and in July of 1922 George Dennis Barnett passed away at the age of 58.

Aerial view of the New Cathedral, with Rosati-Kain High School to the east

Courtesy of Archdiocese of St. Louis Archives

Rosati-Kain High School

Henry P. Hess (1884–1959), architect

Photograph by John C. Guenther, FAIA, LEED AP

Ravenna Mosaic, St. Louis, Missouri, mosaic sign
Courtesy of Cathedral Basilica of Saint Louis Museum

1923: Ravenna Mosaics, Inc.

With the first three mosaic projects completed, Emi Frei, Sr. proposed to Archbishop Glennon that he form an international team of the very best artists and craftsmen to design and install mosaics for his cathedral. With the opportunity for ample work, Frei could offer a collaborative arrangement —the stability and local presence of his St. Louis firm coupled with the tremendous capabilities and expertise of a foreign office well-known for design and production, resulting in an economy of scale.

The Berlin firm of Pühl & Wagner, with Gottfried Heinersdorff, known by Frei for some time, offered the ideal collaboration to realize the large-scale mosaic work in the Byzantine-Romanesque style.

Given Archbishop Glennon's goal of completing as much of the cathedral's mosaics as possible in time for the centenary celebration of the founding of the Diocese of St. Louis (July 18, 1826), he agreed to Frei's proposal. Favorable factors included depressed postwar German labor wages, an established reputation for Byzantine designs by Pühl & Wagner, and efficient production given the size of the new organization.

In 1923, Emil Frei, Sr. incorporated Ravenna Mosaics, Inc. in St. Louis, serving as owner and president, and providing the projects and leadership for the US market. He chose the name Ravenna Mosaics in honor of its history as the center of Byzantine mosaics.

Emil Frei, Sr. (1869–1942)
Courtesy of Emil Frei & Associates, Inc.

Paul Heuduck (1882–1972)
Courtesy of Cathedral Basilica of Saint Louis Museum

To further establish this business relationship, Frei's son, Emil Frei, Jr., spent nine months in 1923 in Berlin and Munich at the Pühl & Wagner workshop and at the Emil Frei branch office in Munich. August Wagner sent Paul Heuduck, one of his experienced mosaic craftsmen, to the St. Louis branch to install the mosaics fabricated in Berlin for the Cathedral of Saint Louis. Heuduck facilitated the coordination of this project between the workshops on two continents.

1923: The First Byzantine Mosaics

Considered to be the preeminent mosaic artist of his time, Professor August Oetken (1868–1951), a Berlin artist and educator, was selected to develop George Barnett's vision for the transepts after Barnett's passing from pneumonia in July 1922.

Oetken, who had designed mosaics for more than 20 years with Pühl & Wagner, designed the transept arcade mosaics from his Berlin home in 1922. Oetken visited in November 1923 to see the mosaics installed within the cathedral. During his three-month stay, he created more designs. Of note, Oetken would provide designs for eight different commissions for the New Cathedral.

Paul Heuduck began with the red-and-gold designs in the transept arcades supporting the gallery level. The transept arcades, completed by Ravenna Mosaics, Inc. in November of 1923, were well received and considered a great success. They were an impressive start to the next phase of mosaic work.

Archbishop Glennon commissioned Emil Frei, Sr. to develop a thematic plan for the entire cathedral. On December 6, 1923, Frei completed a 16-page general plan for the mosaic decoration. It was submitted to the theological advisors of the archbishop for review and comment.

East transept architrave mosaics (1922–23). Photograph by Serhii Chrucky © Serhii Chrucky I Esto

1924: The Arch of Triumph

The General Plan of Mosaic Decoration was finalized in early 1924 by the archbishop's theological advisors and Emil Frei, Sr. The themes and designs for the arches supporting the central dome were approved by Archbishop Glennon.

By November of 1924, three more mosaics were completed. The impressive Arch of Triumph is the north arch under the main dome and most visible when facing the altar. The Byzantine mosaic has Christ enthroned at the apex, with Old Testament saints to His left and New Testament and recent saints to His right.

Felix Baumhauer (1876–1960), a Munich-based artist associated with Pühl & Wagner, designed the Arch of Triumph. The soffit arch underneath—the Arch of Priesthood—is highly visible to the priests seated in the sanctuary of the cathedral and directly above the archbishop's throne and presider's chair.

Completing this composition, August Oetken designed the two pendentives, triangle-shaped areas that flank the Arch of Triumph, during his three-month stay in early 1924. The pendentives symbolically depict angels as the synagogue (Old Testament), with veiled eyes, on the right, and the Church (New Testament), clearly seeing the truths of faith, on the left. Paul Heuduck and Ravenna Mosaics, Inc. installed the mosaics in 1924.

Arch of Triumph, soffit under Arch of Triumph, and two pendentives (1924). Photograph by Serhii Chrucky © Serhii Chrucky I Esto

Top left, Arch of Triumph sketch. Felix Baumhauer (1876–1960), artist. Courtesy of Saint Louis University Archives. Top middle, Arch of Triumph color maquette by artist Felix Baumhauer. Courtesy of Cathedral Basilica of Saint Louis Archives. Top right, Arch of Triumph by artist Felix Baumhauer, installed in 1924 by Ravena Mosaics, Inc. Photograph by Serhii Chrucky © Serhii Chrucky I Esto

1924: The Art of Mosaics

The art of mosaics begins with the artist, who follows a process of development and realization. The artist prepares a design sketch of the subject matter, according to the patron's commission. With the approval of the sketch, the design is modified until it is approved. An enlarged watercolor is then prepared and submitted for review and approval of the design and composition by the patron and their advisors. A final enlarged watercolor is then prepared for the mosaicist to translate into the mosaic medium and into the actual scale of the medium. The full-size "cartoon" of the mosaic design is then cut up into manageable sections for the mosaics to be applied, in reverse and face down, onto paper sheets, to then be applied to the final location in a wet bed of mortar. The glass tesserae, composed of gold leaf and colors, are tapped into place, with slight angles to capture and reflect the light, producing a shimmering effect. When secure, the paper is removed and the mosaics are cleaned and grouted.

Mosaicists interpret designs from full-scale cartoons.

Courtesy of Saint Louis University Libraries Special Collections

Moses mosaic

Courtesy of Cathedral Basilica of Saint Louis Museum

1925: August Oetken and Commissions for the Centennial

With the three large mosaics completed in 1924, Archbishop Glennon then approved 11 smaller mosaics. These were followed by six more large mosaics in 1925—an immense undertaking.

There were several reasons for such a large number of mosaic works. First, Pühl & Wagner needed work and were willing to fabricate the mosaics in Berlin at minimum cost to keep the business in operation. In addition, Monsignor Tannrath, cathedral rector overseeing the cathedral mosaic project, wanted as much completed as possible before the archbishop's return from Europe. Lastly, 1926 marked the centennial anniversary of the diocese's creation, with major celebrations planned, including the consecration of the cathedral. Archbishop Glennon hoped for a more finished cathedral.

Mosaics commissioned in 1925 and designed by Oetken included:

1. The Sanctuary Soffit Arch framing the north rose window, which featured a decorative pattern with seraphim and was completed in early 1925.
2. The Beatitudes on the Arcades of the Nave featured eight angels holding scrolls of the Beatitudes surrounded by a scrollwork of vines on a blue background, which was completed in July 1925.
3. The pendentives in the Sanctuary Dome of Doctors of the Church with two of the doctors, St. Thomas and St. Ambrose, facing the nave, were finished before August 1925.

St. Ambrose pendentive

Sanctuary Dome (August 1925), August Oetken

Photograph by Sam Fentress © SAM FENTRESS PHOTOGRAPHY

The Beatitudes (July 1925), August Oetken

Photograph by Sam Fentress © SAM FENTRESS PHOTOGRAPHY

4. The Arch of Creation in the east transept was designed by Oetken and was completed by August 1925.
5. The Arch of Sanctification in the west transept was designed by Oetken and was completed in December 1925.
6. The All Souls Chapel was begun in August 1925 and was finished by Christmas of 1925. The mosaic inlay for the altar was delayed and installed by Easter 1926, just prior to the consecration of the cathedral that summer. Rudolf Scheffler (1884–1973), a German artist and gifted designer of Pühl & Wagner, emigrated to the United States in 1924 and designed the mosaics, altar, and statuary for the All Souls Chapel. The chapel was a gift by St. Louis lawyer John S. Leahy. The chapel altar was a gift of Anna S. Meagher.

The major mosaic commissions from 1923 to 1925 were fabricated in Berlin by Pühl & Wagner, with some of the minor commissions done in St. Louis and New York.

The commission for the transept arches in 1923 led to 10 major commissions and more than a dozen minor commissions prior to the centennial celebration and consecration of the cathedral on June 29, 1926.

Maquette of Arch of Sanctification
August Oetken (1925)
Courtesy of Cathedral Basilica of Saint Louis Archives

Mosaicist installs tesserae on the cartoon.
Courtesy of Archdiocese of St. Louis Archives

Arch of Sanctification and The Ascension (December 1925)
August Oetken
Photograph by Serhii Chrucky © Serhii Chrucky I Esto

East transept, ca. 1940

Photographer unknown

Courtesy of Archdiocese of St. Louis Archives

Resurrection painting in east transept (1924)

Photographer: Jack J. Zehrt. *St. Louis Globe-Democrat*, March 28, 1948

From the collections of the St. Louis Mercantile Library, University of Missouri–St. Louis

1924–25: The First Transept Paintings

Conrad Schmitt Studios of Milwaukee, Wisconsin, received the commission for the mosaic-paintings of the east and west transept half domes and arch soffits (the underpart of the arch).

Towering above the east transept of the Cathedral of Saint Louis was one of the country's most outstanding reproductions of the Resurrection. Executed by Conrad Schmitt Studios, the al secco (wet-on-dry plaster treatment) mosaic-painting was titled *Resurrexit Sicut Dixit* ("He is risen as He said."—Matthew 28:6). The soffits, or underpart of the arch, of the east arch were also part of the commission. The west transept painting represented the Ascension of Christ into heaven.

The artist was Gotthard Bauer of Munich. After carefully studying the works of August Oetken and Felix Baumhauer as they were being installed on the Arch of Triumph, the Arch of Creation, and the Arch of Sanctification in the mid-1920s, Bauer executed the east and west transept half domes and arch soffits in the same style. They were the only large artworks in the cathedral not to be in mosaics, remaining in place from 1924 until 1984, when water damage led to the decision to remove and replace them with mosaics.

The Resurrection al secco mosaic-painting covers 2,500 square feet within the half dome, over 70 feet above the cathedral floor. The figure of Christ is 12 feet tall, and the children in the smaller center circle are 8 feet tall.

1924–25: Al Secco Method

The al secco mosaic-paintings in the east and west transepts, along with the areas surrounding the north and south rose windows, were designed and installed by Conrad Schmitt Studios in the Cathedral of Saint Louis from 1924 to 1925.

In a 1937 article, Conrad Schmitt described the al secco method involving the preparation of the plaster surface being "coated with pure lime, water, and casein. Then casein, pure earth colors, and lime are mixed, keeping the wall moist during the application of the color. In the drying process, oxygen causes a film to form on the surface, which is the secret of its enduring qualities. This method of fresco-secco . . . is durable, resistant to industrial gasses and atmospheric changes and will bear washing."

It has been said that alfresco was "the only painting that Michelangelo thought worthy of man."

In 1921, $250,000 was given to the Archdiocese by Mrs. Katherine Manan McBride to build McBride High School in St. Louis as a memorial to her husband, William Cullen McBride, an outstanding Catholic layman. In the words of the late Cardinal Glennon, Mr. McBride was "a man who saw and understood the questions of his day, and even foresaw those of the future. He realized the need for educating the hearts and minds of youth so as to fit them for facing the problems of life."

McBride High School was a three-story, colonnaded limestone building designed by Henry P. Hess, architect, and located at 1901 Kingshighway at the corner of Kingshighway and Easton (later renamed Martin Luther King Drive). Under the guidance of the Brothers of Mary, McBride opened in 1925. During its 47 years, McBride rose to become a landmark and a milestone in education, molding and shaping the lives of 600 young men each year and preparing them to meet their moral and civic responsibilities in an adult world. For a variety of reasons, the school closed in 1971.

Mural depicting adoration of the Trinity above the High Altar, St. Louis Cathedral, St. Louis Missouri

Designed and installed by Conrad Schmitt Studios, ca.1926

From *Church Property Administration*, November 1937 issue. Courtesy of Conrad Schmitt Studios Archives

McBride High School (1925), architect Henry P. Hess (1884–1959)

Courtesy of Archdiocese of St. Louis Archives

Interior view of Scheffler's scale model illustrating Oetken's designs for the two forward domes

Courtesy of Saint Louis University Archives

Scheffler's scale model at the Chicago exposition in 1926

Courtesy of Saint Louis University Archives

1926: Mosaic Master Plan

With the belief that the commissions would continue for the three domes, the two transept half domes, some pendentives, the vestibules, the sanctuary gallery walls, and the walls under the southern dome, Ravenna Mosaics had the artist Rudolph Scheffler build a scale model of the cathedral in order to show mosaics completed and the designs for those remaining. The model made in 1925 or early 1926 was exhibited at an exposition in Chicago in 1926. Of note, the model contained the only known representations of August Oetken's unexecuted designs for the central dome and sanctuary dome.

Although these designs remained unrealized, they illustrate the beauty and composition of Oetken's Byzantine mosaic designs, inspired by his studies of the fifth- and sixth-century mosaics in Ravenna.

Oetken's design for the central dome is similar to the General Plan of Mosaic Decoration from 1923 prepared by Emil Frei, Sr.

For the Dome of the Apostles, directly above the altar and baldacchino, Frei planned for the dome to be encircled with the Twelve Apostles. In Oetken's design, each Apostle is standing beneath a palm tree.

The central dome covered 10,860 square feet, while the Dome of the Apostles covered 2,700 square feet. The two domes covered an area of 13,500 square feet—almost equal to all work prior to 1926 by Ravenna Mosaics.

Given the number of major projects completed in rapid succession, Archbishop Glennon decided to wait to commission the domes. The pace of installation slowed.

June 29, 1926: Cathedral Consecrated

Archbishop Glennon selected June 29, 1926, for the consecration of the cathedral. This year was significant as it was the centennial of the creation of the Diocese of Saint Louis.

John Cardinal Bonzano, the Papal Legate to the Eucharistic Congress, represented His Holiness, Pope Pius XI. He led an impressive assemblage of prelates including Michael Cardinal Faulhaber of Munich, Germany; Patrick Cardinal Hayes of New York; and Patrick Cardinal O'Donnell of Armaugh, Primate of All Ireland. Fifty thousand persons greeted the arriving dignitaries at Lindell and Union Boulevards.

After Archbishop Glennon consecrated the high altar and his four suffragan bishops consecrated the four chapel altars simultaneously, the ushers opened the cathedral at 10 a.m., with the multitude rushing into every non-reserved pew and the galleries above.

Fifty-nine archbishops and bishops, 1,000 priests, and countless members of religious orders processed into the cathedral, followed by the four cardinals and Archbishop Glennon. Monsignor J. J. Tannrath read the greetings of Pope Pius XI. Cardinal Bonzano sang the Pontifical Mass. Cardinal Hayes preached.

That evening, thousands of parochial school students and teachers and members of the Catholic societies lined Lindell Boulevard as the prelates processed with the Blessed Sacrament. More than 100,000 spectators gathered as the prelates left the cathedral and processed to the archbishop's residence at 4510 Lindell Boulevard, and then to the Sacred Heart Convent on Taylor and Maryland Avenues. The great and holy day came to a close with the singing of the hymn "Holy God, We Praise Thy Name."

Consecration of the Cathedral of Saint Louis on June 29, 1926

Courtesy of Archdiocese of St. Louis Archives

Archbishop Glennon greets Cardinal Bonzano, Apostolic Delegate to the Eucharistic Congress of Chicago in June 1926.

Cardinal Bonzano came to St. Louis for the dedication of the Cathedral of Saint Louis, June 29, 1926.

From *The Great St. Louis Cathedral* by William B. Faherty, SJ (1988). Courtesy of Archdiocese of St. Louis Archives

Indian Ceiling (1927–28)
Adjacent to All Souls Chapel

Photograph by John C. Guenther, FAIA, LEED AP

Entrance to All Souls Chapel (1927–28)

Photograph by John C. Guenther, FAIA, LEED AP

Ambulatory ceiling (1927–28) along the front of the nave, just inside the door from the vestibule

Photograph by John C. Guenther, FAIA, LEED AP

1927–28: Ambulatory Ceilings

Rather than move forward with mosaics for the domes in 1927, Archbishop Glennon commissioned Ravenna Mosaics, Inc. to design and install the side entrances and ambulatories—the passages between the chapels and the nave columns.

The ceiling of the ambulatory along the front of the nave, just inside the door from the entrance vestibule, and the ambulatory ceiling alongside the All Souls Chapel were commissioned.

Both of these ceilings are very distinctive in their geometric patterns. The south ambulatory ceiling features large fish caught in nets. The east ambulatory ceiling features a vibrant Native American pattern, with the design attributed by some to Rudolf Scheffler, who designed the All Souls Chapel two years prior. Both commissions were completed in early 1928.

The southwest, northwest, and southeast corridor entrances in marble then received mosaics with geometric decorative border inlays, which were added in 1928.

Vestibule mosaics (1929–31)
John Von Wicht (1891–1982) designed the vestibule mosaics on the life of King St. Louis IX.
Courtesy of Archdiocese of St. Louis Archives

King St. Louis IX mosaics
Photograph by John C. Guenther, FAIA, LEED AP

1927–31: Vestibule Transformation

In 1927, discussions to proceed with mosaics for the vestibule began between Ravenna Mosaics and Monsignor J. J. Tannrath, rector of the cathedral, chancellor of the archdiocese, and supervisor of the mosaic work. The first design by Rudolf Scheffler in 1927 was ornate and proved too expensive. The Great Depression that began in 1929 delayed the project further.

Sadly, Monsignor Tannrath died in June of 1929. Without any immediate family surviving him, he left his estate to his friend, Archbishop Glennon, who in turn honored him by bequeathing the estate to commission the vestibule mosaics and dedicating them to Monsignor Tannrath.

In 1929, John Von Wicht, a German artist who had emigrated to the US in 1923 and was with Ravenna Mosaics (New York branch since 1925) was selected to create a new design in a simplified Byzantine style. His design was refined numerous times before receiving Archbishop Glennon's approval on February 23, 1931. The design featured 10 scenes from the life of King St. Louis IX, images of the four evangelists and Christ, and a Christogram.

The original bare brick box vestibule with a high flat ceiling terminating in dark corners was transformed architecturally into a barrel vault ceiling, with the curved gold tesserae mosaic surface reflecting the maximum amount of light through the three existing transom windows to the viewer.

The mosaics, fabricated by Pühl & Wagner in Berlin, were completed by June 27, 1931. The 3,500-square-foot vestibule project marked the end of the second phase of mosaic work at the cathedral. As the Great Depression set in, the next mosaic installation was not executed until after the World War II—a lull of 15 years.

Vestibule mosaics
Photograph by John C. Guenther, FAIA, LEED AP

1929–31: Saint Louis Preparatory Seminary

In 1931, the first Saint Louis Preparatory Seminary, the present Kenrick-Glennon Seminary building, opened on the same spacious grounds as the second Kenrick. This facility hosted classes for the last two years of high school and four full years of college. Formation was provided by the Vincentians.

Henry P. Hess (1884–1959) was the architect for the Saint Louis Preparatory Seminary. Hess, born in St. Louis in 1884, worked for the St. Louis architectural firms of Isaac S. Taylor, Eames & Young, and William B. Ittner. Hess opened his own firm in 1916. His first independent commission was St. Rose's School on Goodfellow Street. Upon its completion, he became a favorite architect of John Joseph Cardinal Glennon, an enthusiastic supporter of school construction. Until his death in 1959, Hess received many commissions for school buildings within the Archdiocese of St. Louis and elsewhere in the Midwest, completing approximately 700 structures. In addition to designing Kenrick-Glennon Seminary (previously Cardinal Glennon College, originally Saint Louis Preparatory Seminary), Hess also designed Rosati-Kain High School at Lindell and Newstead, McBride High School at North Kingshighway and Cote Brilliante, Christian Brothers College at Clayton Road and DeMun (in Clayton), and Mary Queen of Peace complex at West Lockwood near Berry in Webster Groves.

Saint Louis Preparatory Seminary construction in 1931
Courtesy of the Archdiocese of St. Louis Office of Archives

Courtyard entrance to St. Joseph's Chapel, Saint Louis Preparatory Seminary, now Kenrick-Glennon Seminary
Photograph by John C. Guenther, FAIA, LEED AP

Tower and dome
Saint Louis Preparatory Seminary, now Kenrick-Glennon Seminary
Photograph by John C. Guenther, FAIA, LEED AP

Ordination of 20 Kenrick Seminary graduates into priesthood, 1938
St. Louis Globe-Democrat Collection, from the collections of the St. Louis Mercantile Library, University of Missouri– St. Louis

1938: Ordination

Twenty Kenrick Seminary graduates were among those ordained into the priesthood, along with subdeacons, in a service at the Cathedral of Saint Louis on Saturday, June 11, 1938.

Rendering of rectory for New Cathedral
O'Meara & Hills, architects; G. E. Quick, associate architect
Courtesy of Cathedral Basilica of Saint Louis Archives

Dr. Mario Salvador (1917–99)
Courtesy of Cathedral Basilica of Saint Louis Archives

1940–41: Rectory

Plans for the rectory for the Cathedral of Saint Louis were first announced on January 3, 1938, by the pastor, Very Reverend Nicholas W. Brinkman. Originally, the rectory was in a three-story house where the cathedral parish school is located. The priests then made their home across the street on Newstead and Maryland Avenues. For 21 years, the clergy staff resided at 4371 Lindell Boulevard, in a residence purchased in 1916.

The rectory for the New Cathedral was designed by O'Meara & Hills, architects, of St. Louis, Missouri; Detroit, Michigan; and Minneapolis, Minnesota, with G. E. Quick, associate architect, using the gray granite, green roof tiles, and architectural details found in the great Cathedral of Saint Louis alongside. The rectory was completed in 1941.

Patrick M. O'Meara, born in 1890 and educated at Notre Dame (1909–10), joined James B. Hills in partnership, forming the architectural firm of O'Meara & Hills, St. Louis, Missouri, and St. Paul, Minnesota, which established a reputation as specialists in Roman Catholic ecclesiastical work.

In addition to their design for the rectory of the Cathedral of Saint Louis, they also designed Villa Duchesne for the Ladies of the Sacred Heart, the White House Retreat Center for the Society of Jesus, the Church of St. James the Greater, De Paul Hospital for the Daughters of Charity of St. Vincent de Paul, St. Wenceslaus Church, and the monastery for the Carmelite Sisters.

Dr. Mario Salvador, age 23, arrived in 1940 to become the second director of music, organist, and choir director for the Cathedral of Saint Louis (1940–92). He assumed his post on October 1, 1940. He succeeded the late Professor William Theodore Diebels, who died on May 28, 1940, after a service of 23-and-a-half years at the cathedral.

He served in the US Army during World War II. Upon his discharge in 1946, he returned to St. Louis, where his recitals filled the cathedral, especially for the organ dedication in 1949 and rededication in 1984. His choirs included men and boys and a priest choir.

In October 1941, Paul Heuduck became sole owner of the Ravenna Company, which was at that time inactive and would not work again until the end of the war, when the installation of mosaics was undertaken to complete the interiors. Ravenna Mosaics continued to be located in the St. Louis studio and offices of Emil Frei at 3934 South Grand Avenue until 1949.

1943: Military Memorial Mass

Founded by three Christian Brothers who arrived in St. Louis and founded their first school just west of the Old Cathedral, the Cathedral Male Free School was opened on September 11, 1849, to 200 grade school boys. A new and more permanent school followed on 8th and Cerre Streets in 1855. By 1882, a new school opened at Kingshighway and Easton Avenue (now Martin Luther King Drive). Following a tragic fire there on October 5, 1916, the property was sold, and the school and campus were moved to Clayton Road in 1922.

In 1934, Christian Brothers College (CBC) negotiated an agreement with the United States Army to introduce the Junior Reserve Officer Training Corps (JROTC) to the school's curriculum.

Fourteen hundred CBC men served in the armed forces during World War II. Forty CBC alums made the ultimate sacrifice. The JROTC program lasted nearly 60 years and remains an important part of the school's history and identity.

Christian Brothers College alumni killed in service in World War II were honored with a military Mass at the Cathedral of Saint Louis on November 4, 1943.

Parents of those killed, members of the Fathers' Club, the faculty, and the entire CBC Cadet Corps held a one-minute salute.

1943 military memorial Mass

St. Louis Globe-Democrat Collection, from the collections of the St. Louis Mercantile Library, University of Missouri–St. Louis

Members of the CBC Junior Reserve Officer Training Corps (JROTC)

Courtesy of Christian Brothers College High School, St. Louis

Christian Brothers College High School (CBC), Clayton Road campus at DeMun (1922–2003)

Henry P. Hess (1884–1959), architect

Courtesy of Christian Brothers College High School, St. Louis

Archbishop Glennon waves from his TWA flight to his last visit to the Holy See (1946).

Courtesy of Archdiocese of St. Louis Archives

Archbishop Amleto Cicognani, Apostolic Delegate, presided over the solemn Mass.

Courtesy of Archdiocese of St. Louis Archives

1946: Cardinal Glennon Returns Home

With the passing of John Kain (1841–1903), the archbishop of St. Louis, on October 13, 1903, John Joseph Glennon (1862–1946), although only 41 years old, was appointed to succeed him. Over his 43-year tenure, the venerable Glennon led his archdiocese through World War I, the Great Depression, and World War II.

On Christmas Eve 1945, it was announced that the 83-year-old Glennon was to be elevated to the College of Cardinals. Although he thought himself too old to make the journey to Rome, he eventually joined fellow cardinals-elect Francis Spellman and Thomas Tien Ken-sin. On their flight, he contracted a cold from which he would not recover. Pope Pius XII elevated him to cardinal priest of San Clemente al Laterano in the consistory on February 18, 1946.

On his return trip to the United States, Glennon stopped in his native Ireland. While in Dublin, he was diagnosed with uremic poisoning. He was received by President Seán T. O'Kelly and Taoiseach Éamon de Valera. He died on March 9, 1946, in Dublin, where he had been triumphantly welcomed on his way back home from Rome with the Red Hat. The cardinal's body was returned to St. Louis and buried at the Cathedral.

As St. Louisans recall, their beloved cardinal never returned. St. Louis had prepared to welcome its first cardinal, Archbishop Glennon. Lindell Boulevard was illuminated for the parade that would never be. Archbishop Glennon's funeral was held on March 16, 1946, with one of the largest crowds ever to gather at the New Cathedral of St. Louis. Archbishop Amleto Cicognani, Apostolic Delegate, presided over the solemn Mass.

1946: A New Vision

Joseph Elmer Ritter (1892–1967) was appointed archbishop of St. Louis by Pope Pius XII—the fourth archbishop of the Archdiocese of St. Louis—on July 20, 1946, succeeding the late Cardinal John J. Glennon. On October 8, 1946, about 6,000 people witnessed the installation of Archbishop Ritter.

His stewardship of the Archdiocese came at a time when St. Louis was the eighth-largest city in the United States, with a population of 856,796 (an all-time peak) in 1950, composed of ethnic Germans, Irish, English, Scots, Italians, and Eastern Europeans, along with African Americans from the rural South, traveling north in great numbers and making up almost 17 percent of the city's population.

With the problem of racism in St. Louis, one of Ritter's first acts marked his tenure as archbishop with its courage and decency. In 1946, his first year in St. Louis, he instructed all pastors in the archdiocese to end racial segregation in the parochial schools. Archbishop Ritter would go on to order St. Louis Catholic schools to be desegregated in 1947. The US Supreme Court would not take the same action with the nation's public schools until 1954.

Archbishop Ritter also set three goals for continuing to improve the cathedral: to add a sacristy to the north, to improve the mechanical systems, and to complete the mosaics.

Pontifical High Mass for the installation of Archbishop Joseph Elmer Ritter on October 8, 1946, as successor to John Cardinal Glennon

St. Louis Globe-Democrat Collection, from the collections of the St. Louis Mercantile Library, University of Missouri–St. Louis

About 6,000 people witnessed the installation of Archbishop Joseph Elmer Ritter on October 8, 1946, as successor to John Cardinal Glennon.

St. Louis Globe-Democrat Collection, from the collections of the St. Louis Mercantile Library, University of Missouri– St. Louis

Joseph Elmer Ritter (1892–1967)

Fourth archbishop of the Archdiocese of St. Louis. Courtesy of Archdiocese of St. Louis Archives

1947: Hildreth Meière

Hildreth Meière (1892–1961), an American muralist, was well-known for her Art Deco designs. During her 40-year career she completed approximately 100 commissions, including the iconic interiors at the Nebraska State Capitol; the dynamic roundels of Dance, Drama, and Song at Radio City Music Hall; and the apse and narthex mosaics and stained glass windows at St. Bartholomew's Episcopal Church in Manhattan. She was an influential practitioner in American liturgical art, and one of the preeminent mosaicists in the history of American art.

Meière's first commission for the Cathedral of Saint Louis in 1945 was to design Byzantine-style glass mosaics for the soffit of the eastern arch supporting the yet-undecorated north dome with the Sacrifices of Abraham and Isaac and Melchizedek, above the east sanctuary wall of the Passover mosaic, which would not be installed until 1967. The east arch soffit mosaics were commissioned by George John Maguolo, fabricated by Pühl & Wagner Studios in Berlin, and installed by the Ravenna Company in 1947.

Robert E. Harmon (1915–99), a graduate of Washington University, joined the Emil Frei, Inc. studio in 1938. Favoring modern design, he became a prolific member of the studio artists, rising to prominence with his early collaboration with Emil Frei, Jr. on St. Mark's Episcopal Church in 1938.

In 1947, Harmon became the studio's chief designer. That same year, the west soffit arch in the sanctuary designed by Harmon was installed at the same time as Meière's east soffit arch. Harmon was blessed with an incredibly long career.

Sanctuary eastern soffit arch (1945–46). Hildreth Meière, artist. Pühl & Wagner Studios in Berlin. Ravenna Company

Courtesy of International Hildreth Meière Association

Detail of the Nativity, west arch soffit, above the Last Supper mosaic

Robert Harmon, artist, 1947

Photograph courtesy of Emil Frei & Associates

Detail of Abraham and Isaac, east arch soffit, above the Passover mosaic

Hildreth Meière, artist, 1947

Photograph by Sam Fentress © SAM FENTRESS PHOTOGRAPHY

New Kilgen organ. The console is Byzantine in design to conform with the architecture of the cathedral.

Photograph by F. D. Hampson Commercial Photo Co., Inc., St. Louis

St. Louis Globe-Democrat Collection, from the collections of the St. Louis Mercantile Library at University of Missouri–St. Louis

Dedication of the Kilgen liturgical organ at the Cathedral of Saint Louis, under the direction of Mario Salvador, music director, cathedral organist, and choir director, on October 30, 1949

Photograph by F. D. Hampson. Courtesy of Archdiocese of St. Louis Archives

Baldacchino and organ screen behind, ca. 1949

Courtesy of Cathedral Basilica of Saint Louis Archives

1949: The New Kilgen Organ

The new $100,000 Kilgen organ was dedicated on Sunday evening, October 30, 1949, at 8 p.m. The blessing was given by Archbishop Joseph E. Ritter. Dr. Mario Salvador, the second director of music, organist, and choir director for the Cathedral of Saint Louis (1940–92), performed the dedication recital for an audience of more than 3,000. Dr. Salvador designed and planned the organ over a three-year period in collaboration with Eugene Kilgen, president of the Kilgen Organ Company. The four-manual console is Byzantine in design to conform with the architecture of the cathedral. The new organ was the largest built for any cathedral in the world since World War II.

According to the Cathedral Basilica of Saint Louis, this was a culmination of planning efforts that began on September 18, 1946, when contracts were signed for a new Kilgen organ behind the main altar, with 77 ranks of pipes, including 14 stops from the 1915 organ. The cost was $34,375 and the old organ!

On May 27, 1948, contracts were signed for the processional organ, located in the south gallery. The organ consisted of 10 ranks of pipes on a two-manual console. It is also playable from the main organ. The instrument was previously the Echo Organ in Carnegie Hall, New York City. The total cost was $9,825.

The main organ console and choir were hidden behind the altar, with the organ behind the choir. On the main floor level, the swell organ chamber and choir were to the left, while the choir organ chamber and choir were to the right. On the upper level, the great organ chamber was located to the left, while the solo organ chamber was located to the right. The processional organ and console were located more than 300 feet away, in the south gallery, just below the south blue rose window. The four-manual console controls both the grand and the processional organs. With a 150-foot flexible cable attached, the grand organ can be moved to the front of the sanctuary for recitals.

Of note, Eugene Kilgen was the seventh generation of his family to have built organs since Sebastian Kilgen, a Huguenot, built an organ in 1640.

1951: Pontifical Boys' Choir

Archbishop Joseph E. Ritter celebrated a solemn Pontifical Mass for the 25th anniversary of the consecration of the Cathedral of Saint Louis on Sunday, October 14, 1951. Dr. Mario Salvador directed the Cathedral Choir for the 11 a.m. Mass and then gave an organ concert at 4 p.m. that day.

Dr. Salvador organized the new Pontifical Boys' Choir at the Cathedral of Saint Louis in October, 1951 as well. The 95 members, ages 9 to 12, were from Catholic parishes in the St. Louis area. Their debut performance was an appearance at the Christmas Choral Pageant sponsored by the *St. Louis Globe-Democrat* at Kiel Auditorium on December 18, 1951.

They also performed at the cathedral's Midnight Mass in 1951 and sung the "Missa Choralis" of Msgr. Licinio Refice, who was the teacher of harmony at the Pontifical School of Sacred Music in Rome, and under whom Dr. Salvador studied.

In addition to these performances, the new Pontifical Boys' Choir was heard only when the archbishop was present.

The New Pontifical Boys' Choir at the Cathedral of Saint Louis rehearses under the direction of Mario Salvador, choir director and organist, on October 8, 1951

St. Louis Globe-Democrat Collection, from the collections of the St. Louis Mercantile Library, University of Missouri–St. Louis

Dr. Mario Salvador reviewing music with members of the New Pontifical Boys' Choir

Photograph by Arteaga Photos LTD. Courtesy of Arteaga Photos LTD. and Mario Salvador Collection, Ruth T. Watanabe Special Collections, Sibley Music Library, Eastman School of Music, University of Rochester

Mario Salvador, music director, cathedral organist, and choir director, at the Kilgen organ
Courtesy of Archdiocese of St. Louis Archives

Far left: The green roof tile was replaced with Ludowici tile roof in 1952.

Courtesy of Archdiocese of St. Louis Office of Building and Real Estate

Left: The exterior restoration in 1952

Courtesy of St. Louis Public Library–Central Library

1952: A Thorough Cleaning and New Roof

In 1952, the Cathedral of Saint Louis underwent its first major renovation in its 45-year history. Work included the cleaning of the exterior, tuck-pointing of the masonry, and replacing of the green-tile roof. The costs were estimated at $400,000 at the time.

The exterior walls of the soft Vermont and New Hampshire granite were cleaned and restored to their original light gray. The magnificent north and south rose windows were covered with plywood to protect the stained glass during the cleaning of the surrounding lacework of the stone.

Many of the granite blocks had cracked under the great weight of the walls. These stones were removed and replaced. The mortar bindings between the stones were tuck-pointed. Cracks caused by settling were repaired. The cathedral was also re-weatherproofed along the joints and windows.

The 50-to-100-pound, green-terra-cotta roof tiles of the central dome, the two towers, the two half domes, and the hip roofs and gable roofs were part of the renovation. Because so many of the roof tiles were cracked and damaged due to weathering, the roof tiles were entirely replaced. The new roof tiles were made with improved casting methods to ensure a longer life. New copper flashing and gutters were installed to ensure proper drainage.

The work was undertaken by Al P. Daly Construction Co., general contractors, and took about one year. The renovation was financed by the archdiocese and members of the cathedral parish under the direction of Archbishop Joseph E. Ritter.

According to J. R. Kearney, Western Waterproofing Company, Inc., in 1952, it was discovered that over the years, airborne smoke, soot, and dirt had gradually accumulated on the exterior of the building. These filthy deposits had not only marred the beauty of the Concord, New Hampshire, granite of which the cathedral is constructed but also had serious corrosive effects on the seams of the stone. Mortar joints were in a critical state of deterioration, permitting penetration of water that had already caused slight damage to the interior mosaics.

With authorization from Archbishop Ritter, work began on the restoration of the weather-damaged structure. The first task was to wash away 38 years of accumulated carbon deposits and dirt on 175,000 square feet of exterior surface. A sand-cleaning method used approximately 280 tons of sand to uncover the gray-white color of the exterior natural stone. Marble on the entrance and sides was carefully washed by hand.

With the exterior cleaned, almost 50 miles of badly weathered mortar joints were replaced with a special expanding type of mortar known as Dilato.

More than 40 men were employed on the cleaning and waterproofing job.

1954: Bishop Rosati Returns

On Sunday, January 1, 1954, at 4 p.m., the Cathedral of Saint Louis Men's Choir and the Pontifical Boys' Choir, along with Archbishop Joseph E. Ritter, appeared in a concert of Christmas music, under the direction of Dr. Mario Salvador in the cathedral.

On June 9, 1954, Mass was held for 1,200 graduates of the Catholic high schools of the Archdiocese of St. Louis in the Cathedral of Saint Louis. Archbishop Ritter officiated and delivered the sermon.

In 1954, Archbishop Ritter petitioned the Congregation of the Mission (Vincentians) in Rome to transfer Bishop Rosati's remains to St. Louis and they agreed.

On Thursday, August 26, 1954, Ritter celebrated the solemn funeral mass and reinterred the remains of St. Louis's first bishop, Joseph Rosati (1789–1843), in the Cathedral of Saint Louis in the crypt below the All Souls Chapel following solemn ceremonies. Bishop Rosati died in Rome in 1843 following a successful mission as Apostolic Delegate to the Republic of Haiti. He had been buried in the Eternal City for more than 100 years.

With the reinternment of Bishop Rosati beneath the crypt of the late Cardinal John J. Glennon, the first and fourth Ordinaries of St. Louis—the "Rome of the West"—were brought together. They were the builders, respectively, of the Old and the New Cathedrals. Both died while on a mission to Rome. Both would lie together from 1954 until 1970, when the remains of Bishop Rosati were moved to his final resting place at the cathedral that he built—the Basilica of St. Louis, King of France, also known as the Old Cathedral.

Archbishop Joseph Ritter celebrated the solemn funeral mass and reinterred the remains of St. Louis's first bishop, Joseph Rosati. Courtesy of Archdiocese of St. Louis Archives

The Cathedral of Saint Louis Men's Choir and the Archbishop Ritter Pontifical Boys' Choir, with Archbishop Joseph E. Ritter, on January 1, 1954

St. Louis Globe-Democrat Collection, from the collections of the St. Louis Mercantile Library, University of Missouri–St. Louis

Mass for 1,200 graduates of the Catholic high schools of the Archdiocese of St. Louis, June 9, 1954

St. Louis Globe-Democrat Collection, from the collections of the St. Louis Mercantile Library, University of Missouri–St. Louis

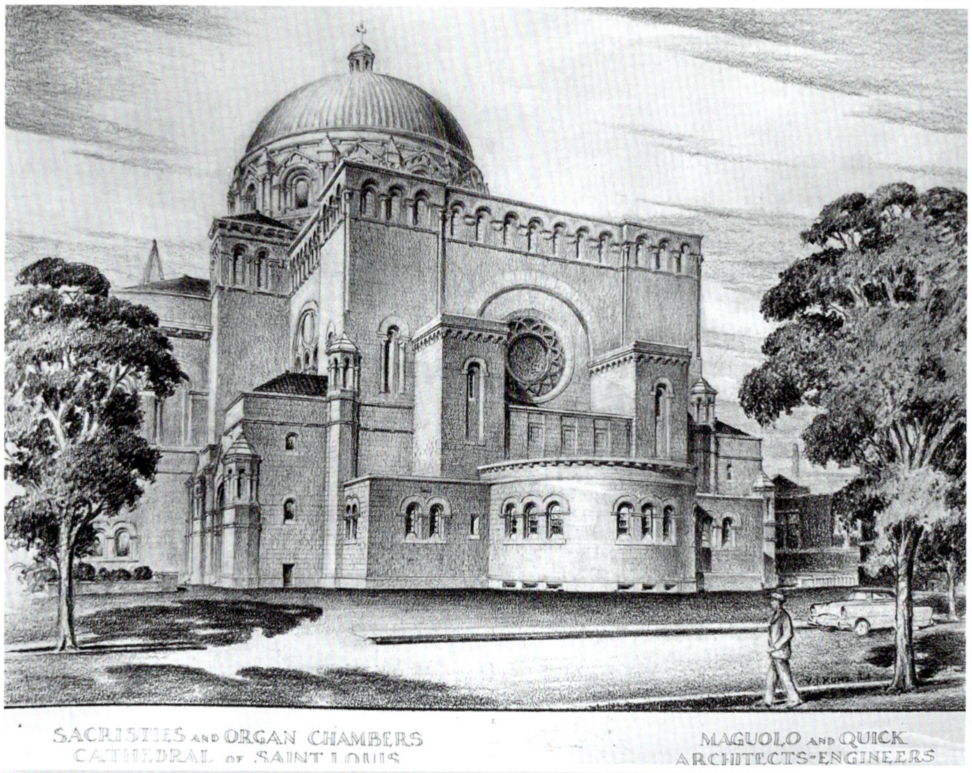

New sacristy and organ chambers

Rendering of design by George John Magualo of the semicircular sacristy, September 9, 1955

Courtesy of Cathedral Basilica of Saint Louis Archives

1955: New Sacristy

After the interruptions to the major work on the mosaics caused by the Great Depression and World War II had passed, the modernization of the cathedral could at last proceed now that the major exterior repair work was completed. On September 9, 1955, Archbishop Joesph E. Ritter announced this major project, whose total cost was estimated to be $1.78 million and that was expected to take several years.

Plans for completing the cathedral included the addition of the sacristy, lighting on both the interior and exterior of the cathedral, and the installation of mosaics on the interior arches and domes.

Lighting was to be modernized, replacing the overloaded and obsolete equipment, and addressing the dimly lit interiors. The new lighting system was to be both practical and artistic, to better light the magnificent mosaics of the interior and floodlight the exterior of the main central dome, the entrance and towers. Sachs Electrical Corporation of St. Louis implemented this work, estimated to cost $260,000 and be completed by the fall of 1956.

With the existing mosaics covering about 35,000 square feet, the remaining areas were designed and installed by the Ravena Company of St. Louis and its associate, the Ravena Company of Berlin.

Approximately 3,000 square feet of mosaic were in process and scheduled to be installed in the small domes on the main level in early 1956. Another 30,000 square feet were planned and designed for the main dome and the two smaller domes in the sanctuary and nave. The estimate for the mosaic work was $870,000.

The original plans in 1906 called for a sacristy behind the altar, but it was dropped due to cost at the time. The proposed semicircular sacristy design by George John Maguolo of Maguolo & G. E. Quick, architects, of St. Louis would extend the cathedral 41 feet to the north. Building was set to begin in 1956.

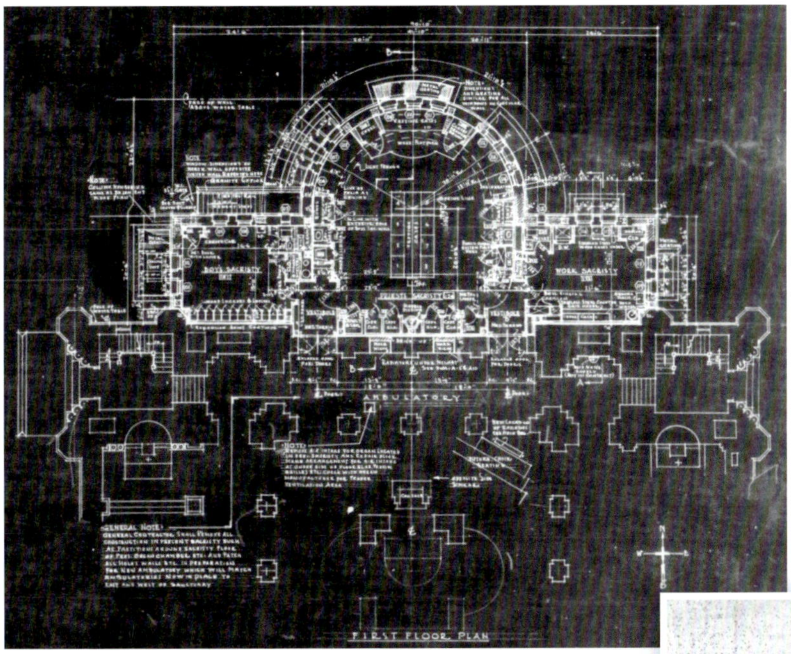

Plan of semicircular sacristy

Maguolo & Quick, architects, June 3, 1955

Courtesy of Archdiocese of St. Louis Building and Real Estate Archives

Elevation of semicircular sacristy, March 18, 1955. Maguolo & Quick, architects, March 18, 1955. Courtesy of Archdiocese of St. Louis Building and Real Estate Archives

1955: George John Maguolo, Architect

George John Maguolo was born in St. Louis on October 11, 1893, to Ferdinand D. and Florina Maguolo. His father was a cabinet worker in Venice, Italy, who emigrated to St. Louis. Maguolo was a graduate in architecture at Washington University, served in World War I, and afterward was chosen to study at the École des Beaux-Arts in Paris. He was principal at O'Meara & Hills, architects, St. Louis, in 1931, working with G. E. Quick at that firm from 1929 to 1944. Maguolo & Quick, architects/engineers, St. Louis, was established in 1945 and operated until 1959, with branch offices in Minneapolis, Detroit, Cincinnati, and Baltimore. Quick died in January of 1960. Maguolo worked on the Cathedral of Saint Louis rectory (completed 1941) and the sacristy (completed 1957). He died on January 4, 1975, in St. Louis.

Cathedral dome lighting fixture, November 2, 1956
Photograph by Piaget
Courtesy of Archdiocese of St. Louis Archives

The semicircular sacristy under construction, April 27, 1956
Photograph by Arteaga Studio
Courtesy of Arteaga Photos LTD.

Cathedral of Saint Louis interior mosaics, November 2, 1956
Courtesy of Archdiocese of St. Louis Archives

1956: Addition and Enhancements

The $400,000 sacristy addition began in 1956, with foundations of reinforced concrete walls installed at the north end of the cathedral, 41 feet into the parking lot, behind the main altar. With the sacristy addition, the overall length of the cathedral totaled 346 feet—longer than any other Catholic cathedral in the US.

The sacristy is composed of five components: a semicircular priests' sacristy; two flanking rectangular wings for the altar boys and sacred vessels; and two towering organ chambers, four stories in height and flanking the north rose window. All of the components were needed architecturally as well as functionally, to blend the relatively low sacristy with the proportions of the great cathedral. Storage facilities were located in the lower level, below the sacristy.

In 1956, a 3,000-pound multi-lamp light, believed to be the largest of its kind in the world, was installed in the cathedral's dome. The 96 sealed-beam projector lamps were designed to send light from the oculus at the center of the dome to the floor 143 feet below in order to illuminate 11,700 square feet of floor and seating space—a little more than one-fourth of an acre. Each lamp had a capacity of 300 watts. Eight specifically designed 1,000-watt "shovel" lights threw out light from the dome to the mosaic surface of the dome itself. The entire multi-lamp unit was controlled by a remotely operated dimmer system, with the dimmer board housed above the main dome and dimmer controls installed in the new sacristy under construction. The $260,000 design by Rambusch Decorating Company of New York was installed by the Sachs Electric Corporation of St. Louis.

One of Ritter's personal priorities was supporting the mission efforts of the Church. St. Louis had played a major role in sending missionaries to the American West, so much that Cardinal Glennon called St. Louis the "Rome of the West," recalling the historic role Rome had played in the evangelization of Europe during the Dark Ages.

In 1956, Ritter sent three priests to work in Bolivia, one of the world's poorest nations. Later, the mission temporarily expanded to a part of Chile.

1957: Addition Completed

The new $500,000 air-conditioned sacristy for the cathedral was completed in May 1957. The granite exterior and scale of the sacristy addition blended beautifully with the massive proportions of the cathedral. The addition included a semicircular priests' sacristy in the center, containing vesting cases for the archbishop, cathedral parish priests, and visiting priests, with altar boys to the west and a work sacristy to the east used by the Altar Society.

The new sacristy replaced the former "sacristy aisle" behind the altar, which was then embellished with marble walls and six mosaic ceiling domes, representing the coats of arms of the bishops, archbishops, and cardinals of St. Louis.

Professor Fritz Bernitzky, a Berlin artist, designed the Domes of the Coat of Arms. The mosaics were fabricated by Wagner Studios in Berlin and installed by the Ravenna Company of St. Louis in 1958.

Eight small domes on the main floor of the cathedral, totaling 3,080 square feet, were commissioned by George John Maguolo (June 1955). Installed by the Ravenna Company in 1957, the design of the domes, by an unknown artist, consisted of geometric patterns and symbols in keeping with the other domes of a similar size and nature on the first floor of the cathedral.

Other work completed included a new tile roof, cleaning and tuck-pointing of the exterior granite walls, and the complete rewiring and relighting of the interior, in order to fully reveal hues, subtle tones, intricate patterns, and interior details of the Cathedral of Saint Louis.

The Pontifical Boys' Choir under the direction of Dr. Mario Salvador sang at the Night Mass on Christmas Day 1957.

St. Louis Globe-Democrat Collection, from the collections of the St. Louis Mercantile Library, University of Missouri–St. Louis

The vesting table allows for six priests to vest for services at one time.

Courtesy of Cathedral Basilica of Saint Louis Archives

Semicircular sacristy completed

The semicircular sacristy designed by George John Maguolo of Maguolo & Quick, architects, was begun February 10, 1956, and completed May 1957 for $345,000.

Courtesy of Cathedral Basilica of Saint Louis Archives

Corridor of Coats of Arms (mosaics installed 1958. Professor Fritz Bernitzky, artist

Photograph by Serhii Chrucky © Serhii Chrucky I Esto

1957: Dome of the Twelve Apostles

In 1956, Hildreth Meière became the first woman honored with the Fine Arts Medal of the American Institute of Architects, having gained the respect of the greatest muralists and architects of her day.

In 1956, Meière was commissioned to design the Dome of the Twelve Apostles and Two Drinking Deer with Meandering Grapevine on the north wall framing the north rose window of the Cathedral of Saint Louis. These mosaic works were commissioned by George John Maguolo of Maguolo & Quick, architect responsible for the ongoing mosaic decoration of the interior, together with Father Thomas Durkin.

For the Byzantine-style Dome of the Twelve Apostles, Meière prepared paper models with both blue and gold backgrounds, as well as models of the other two cathedral domes to better harmonize with the entire scheme. In 1957, Meière asked the Rambusch Studio to "spin" two models in aluminum so that she could study the scale models in gouache on metal for the Dome of the Twelve Apostles.

Her 14-foot-high figures of each of the Twelve Apostles on the dome radiate from a central cross surrounded by four six-winged seraphim. Meière tested 18-foot color cartoons with a 14-foot-high scale figure in place with a banner of an Apostle suspended in the dome. She wanted the Apostles to appear life-size from 100 feet below.

In December 1957, Meière traveled to what had become West Berlin to visit Pühl & Wagner Studios to review the cartoons of the mosaics she had sent ahead to ensure her design, and the proper sequence of the Apostles, would be executed faithfully.

Hildreth Meière, 1957, with an Apostle in the background

Courtesy of Hildreth Meière Family Collection

Hildreth Meière's scale model in gouache on metal for Dome of the Twelve Apostles, Cathedral Basilica of Saint Louis, 1957

Courtesy of International Hildreth Meière Association

Collection of the Cathedral Basilica of Saint Louis

1957: Two Drinking Deer and Meandering Grapevine

In 1957, Hildreth Meière developed her Art Deco–style design for the north wall surrounding the rose window with Two Drinking Deer and Meandering Grapevine, incorporating and relating to the blue background of the Dome of the Twelve Apostles, thus bringing a unifying effect to the sacristy.

The meandering grapevine symbolizes the Eucharist, while the two drinking deer represent the faithful seeking the grace of Christ in the sacrament as they drink in the flowing waters of life, all symbolically alluding to Psalm 42: "As a deer longs for flowing streams, so my soul longs for you, O God."

Meière's design process began with a series of sketches for the north wall with Two Drinking Deer and Meandering Grapevine, first in graphite and then in gouache, followed by a full-scale cartoon for each deer, which required two sheets of 4-foot-wide brown cartoon paper.

Meière's design for the north wall surrounding the rose window with Two Drinking Deer and Meandering Grapevine, scale study in graphite, 1957

Courtesy of the Saint Louis University Archives

Two Drinking Deer and Meandering Grapevine, scale study in gouache, 1957

Courtesy of the Saint Louis University Archives

Full-scale cartoon in gouache for Two Drinking Deer and Meandering Grapevine, 1957 Courtesy of Cathedral Basilica of Saint Louis Archives

Courtesy of International Hildreth Meière Association

Drinking Deer on right side of north wall in glass mosaic, 1958

Courtesy of International Hildreth Meière Association

North wall surrounding rose window with Two Drinking Deer and Meandering Grapevine

Courtesy of International Hildreth Meière Association

Cardinal John Joseph Glennon (1862–1946), archbishop of St. Louis, 1903–46. Coat of Arms In Corridor of Coats of Arms (mosaics installed 1958). Professor Fritz Bernitzky

Photograph by Serhii Chrucky © Serhii Chrucky I Esto

Majolica frieze at base of Drinking Deer on right side of north wall

Courtesy of International Hildreth Meière Association

1958: North Wall

Hildreth Meière made certain that her wall design would be clearly visible from 50 feet below, revealing her attention to naturalistic detail within her stylized Art Deco scheme.

Meière framed her beautiful composition within a series of elaborate, geometric borders, which recalled her Sioux-inspired stepped designs for the rotunda dome of the Nebraska State Capitol (1924–32) and the arch of Temple Emanu-El (1929) in New York City.

Meière's Byzantine-style glass mosaic design for Two Drinking Deer and Meandering Grapevine was fabricated in St. Louis by Ravenna Mosaics, not Berlin. Paul Heuduck obtained tesserae from Italy. The mosaic design was commissioned in 1957 by George John Maguolo and installed in 1958.

The north arch soffit, designed in 1924 by August Oetken, was installed in 1958 above the north rose window and north wall mosaic designed by Hildreth Meière. Meière enhanced and integrated the north arch soffit design, which features the six-winged seraphim incorporated in her design for the Dome of the Twelve Apostles.

1958: A Unified Expression

In 1958, scaffolding was erected in the cathedral's sanctuary in order to install the mosaic designs of Hildreth Meière for the north dome (Dome of the Twelve Apostles) with her 14-foot-high individualized figures radiating from a central cross surrounded by four six-winged seraphim, her designs for the St. Cyril of Jerusalem pendentive and the St. John Chrysostom pendentive below the south half of the Dome of the Twelve Apostles, and her design for Two Drinking Deer and Meandering Grapevine on the north wall framing the north rose window.

Hildreth Meière unified her mosaic designs beautifully, creating a powerful, cohesive expression.

North dome (Dome of the Twelve Apostles) and north wall with Two Drinking Deer and Meandering Grapevine

Courtesy of International Hildreth Meière Association

North dome (Dome of the Twelve Apostles), 1958

Commissioned by George John Maguolo

Medium: Byzantine-style glass mosaic, stained glass

Fabricated by Pühl & Wagner Studios in Berlin

Installed by Ravenna Mosaics

Courtesy of International Hildreth Meière Association

Scaffolding over baldacchino erected for mosaics installation of the Dome of the Twelve Apostles

Courtesy of Cathedral Basilica of Saint Louis Archives

1958: New Pendentives, Dome Mosaics, and Symbolic Windows

The challenge for Meière was to blend her two new pendentives with the other two pendentives, of Thomas and Ambrose, two Doctors of the Church, designed by August Oetken and installed in August 1925.

As she wrote to the head of Pühl & Wagner in Berlin: ". . . it has not been easy to plan the central decorations for the older mosaics, and I have felt that if they disturbed these, they would be wrong, no matter how good in themselves. I only hope that I have succeeded in slipping into place quietly—I am sure I am right in scale, and the color should be sympathetic."

At the same time that she designed the pendentives, Meière designed decoration for the north dome depicting the Twelve Apostles, and the north wall surrounding the rose window with Two Drinking Deer and Meandering Grapevine symbolizing the Eucharist.

She wrote, "I feel that the placing and the subject matter of the remaining spaces gives me far more freedom than those I have just completed."

Hildreth Meière designed stained glass windows separating the figures of the Apostles so that a soft light would enter.

Each window incorporates the symbol of the adjacent Apostle.

Like the glass mosaic of the dome, the windows were fabricated in Berlin by Pühl & Wagner and installed by their American affiliate, Ravenna Mosaics.

Meière described the windows: "I have used only three values, placed at random, so that no set pattern appears, and if there is a variation in the individual glass, so much the better, but the values must be close so that the windows remain a unit."

North dome with the Twelve Apostles; St. Cyril in pendentive on top left; St. John Chrysostom, pendentive on top right; and eastern arch soffit with Melchizedek and Abraham and Isaac on far right

Courtesy of International Hildreth Meière Association

Mosaics for pendentives for Cathedral of Saint Louis prepared in Pühl & Wagner workshop in Berlin, Germany

Courtesy of Cathedral Basilica of Saint Louis Archives

Frieze of acanthus leaves in red, gold, and green majolica (glazed and gilded terra-cotta). The design of the frieze is clearly visible below the Drinking Deer on the north wall.

Courtesy of International Hildreth Meière Association

One-foot-tall majolica frieze with red, white, and green acanthus-leaf pattern forms a continuous border along the arches and bases of the domes

Photograph by Serhii Chrucky © Serhii Chrucky I Esto

One-foot-tall majolica frieze mock-up of corner

Courtesy of Cathedral Basilica of Saint Louis Archives

Photograph by John C. Guenther, FAIA, LEED AP

1958: A Unifying Frieze

The cathedral administrators asked Hildreth Meière to harmonize and unify the existing Byzantine-style glass tesserae created by artists such as John Von Wicht, Felix Baumhauer, August Oetken, and Robert Harmon, and also to incorporate mosaic work in progress and anticipate future mosaic designs harmoniously.

Meière devised a 1-foot-tall frieze of acanthus leaves in red, gold, and green majolica (glazed and gilded terra-cotta)—a continuous border to run along the base of the arches and domes, thus visually unifying the various styles of the existing mosaic decorations within the Cathedral of Saint Louis.

Hildreth Meière was commissioned by George John Maguolo to design the frieze along the base of arches and domes in 1958. The majolica was fabricated by Pühl & Wagner and installed by Ravenna Mosaics.

Saint Frances Cabrini

Courtesy of International Hildreth Meière Association

Saint Isaac Jogues, Saint René Goupil, and Blessed Kateri Tekakwitha

Courtesy of International Hildreth Meière Association

Saint Rose Philippine Duchesne

Courtesy of International Hildreth Meière Association

1959: Pendentives of Saints Who Spread Catholicism in America

Hildreth Meière's final commissions were at the south end of the nave, with her design of four Byzantine-style glass mosaic pendentives supporting the south dome, featuring Saints Who Spread Catholicism in America.

On the southeast pendentive, Meière represented Saint Rose Philippine Duchesne above the Seal of the Religious of the Sacred Heart. In 1818, Mother Rose Philippine Duchesne (1769–1852) and four sisters answered the invitation of Bishop Louis DuBourg (1766–1833) for missionary work in the New World. On September 14, 1818, she opened the Academy of the Sacred Heart in St. Charles, the first tuition-free school west of the Mississippi River.

On the southwest pendentive, Meière depicted Saint Elizabeth Ann Seton (1774–1821), the first US-born saint, above the Seal of the Sisters of Charity of St. Joseph's. Bishop DuBourg, then president of St. Mary's College, Baltimore, served as advisor and spiritual director to Elizabeth Ann Seton, who founded the first American congregation of religious sisters, the Sisters of Charity of St. Joseph's (1809). Its school was the first tuition-free Catholic school in America, marking the start of the Catholic parochial school system in the United States. Seton founded Saint Joseph's Academy and Free School (1810), the first Catholic girls' school in the nation in Emmitsburg, Maryland.

On the northwest pendentive, Meière placed Saint Frances Xavier Cabrini, the first American saint, above the Seal of the Missionary Sisters of the Sacred Heart. Arriving in New York City from Italy in 1889, Cabrini set up schools, hospitals, orphanages, and novitiates across the country. In 1909, the Italian nun became a US citizen.

On the northeast pendentive, Meière depicted Saint Isaac Jogues (1607–46), Saint René Goupil, and Blessed Kateri Tekakwitha above the Seal of the Society of Jesus. Father Isaac Jogues and two lay Jesuits, René Goupil and John Lalande, traveled from France to the New World to evangelize the Indigenous peoples. They, along with five Jesuit priests martyred in Canada in the 1640s, were canonized in 1930 as the eight North American Martyrs—the first and only martyred saints of North America. Saint Kateri Tekakwitha, a Mohawk/Algonquin maiden known for her purity and charity, was born in Canada in 1656. After living a life of sacrifice and persecution by the non-Christian members of her family and tribe, she died of natural causes in Canada in 1680, having remained steadfast in the Catholic faith. She was canonized in 2012.

Meière was commissioned by George John Maguolo to design the four pendentives supporting the south dome. The mosaics were fabricated by Pühl & Wagner in Berlin and installed by Ravenna Mosaics of St. Louis.

1960: Dome of Local History

As Hildreth Meière continued her design for the south end of the nave, known as the Historical Section, her works included the south dome, the pendentives, and the soffits of the arches.

For the Dome of Local History, she designed the 96-foot-high dome with the Seal of the Archdiocese of St. Louis set in a blue field with gold stars of glass tesserae mosaics.

At the center of the dome, she designed the Great Seal of the Archdiocese of Saint Louis, with the seal in the center, surrounded by the fleur-de-lis—a heraldic symbol of St. Louis, set in a field of red-glass tesserae mosaics, bordered by a circular band of a triangular geometric deco pattern, text, and gold rays.

Twelve arched-head leaded clerestory windows, which surround the composition, allow a soft light to enter. Between each window, Meière introduced the stylized Art Deco Meandering Grapevine in gold.

Meière was commissioned by George John Maguolo to design the south dome, Great Seal of the Archdiocese of St. Louis, Stars, and Meandering Grapevine. The Byzantine-style glass mosaics and stained glass were fabricated by Pühl & Wagner in Berlin and installed by Ravenna Mosaics of St. Louis.

South dome—the Dome of Local History

Great Seal of the Archdiocese of St. Louis; Stars; Meandering Grapevine, 1960; south dome arch soffits, 1962

Courtesy of International Hildreth Meière Association

Saints Who Spread Catholicism in America, 1959

South dome pendentives, 1959; south dome, 1960; south dome arch soffits, 1962

Courtesy of International Hildreth Meière Association

1960: A Unifying Approach

Hildreth Meière unified the vast space of the Cathedral of Saint Louis through her design for the south Dome of Local History (1960) and her design for the north Dome of the Twelve Apostles (1958).

Meière's nonfigurative treatment of the centers of the south and north domes in both color and design further unite the Great Seal of the Archdiocese of St. Louis in the center of the south dome and the center of the Dome of the Twelve Apostles with its cross surrounded by four six-winged seraphim.

To further unify the space and designs, Meière repeated a variation of the pattern of the Meandering Grapevine on the walls separating the windows of the south dome, referring back to the wall surrounding the north rose window with Two Drinking Deer and Meandering Grapevine.

For both the north and south domes, Meière designed the leaded windows with three values of glass, placed at random, so that no set pattern appears, and allowing a soft light to enter. The windows, like the glass mosaic dome, were fabricated in Berlin by Pühl & Wagner and installed by their American affiliate, Ravenna Mosaics.

Detail, center of south Dome of Local History (1960)
Courtesy of International Hildreth Meière Association

South Dome of Local History (1960)
Courtesy of International Hildreth Meière Association

Detail, center of north dome (Dome of the Twelve Apostles) (1958)
Courtesy of International Hildreth Meière Association

1960: The Meandering Grapevine

Hildreth Meière incorporated the Meandering Grapevine in her designs for the north wall around the north rose window with Two Drinking Deer and Meandering Grapevine (1958), the south Dome of Local History (1960), and south wall surrounding the south rose window (1962). Each helped to unify the vast interior of the Cathedral of Saint Louis, while Meière designed variations in her stylized Art Deco Meandering Grapevine in gold.

Over time, the Meandering Grapevine has been associated with redemptive themes, such as with the Gospel of John where Jesus proclaims, "I am the vine; you are the branches. If you remain in me and I in you, you will bear much fruit; apart from me you can do nothing."

The grapevine has been symbolic of embodiment of nature's generative power, the cyclical nature of existence, the deity's dominion over life's eternal rhythms, and the Eucharist.

Through Meière's unifying designs, the Byzantine-style glass mosaics envelop all within and communicate quietly and beautifully.

Detail of windows and walls with Meandering Grapevine on south dome (1960)

Courtesy of International Hildreth Meière Association

North wall surrounding rose window with Two Drinking Deer and Meandering Grapevine (1958)

Courtesy of International Hildreth Meière Association

South wall surrounding rose window with variation of Meandering Grapevine (1962)

Courtesy of International Hildreth Meière Association

West Arch Soffit designed by Hildreth Meière (1892–1961) depicting the Educational Apostolate in St. Louis
Photograph by John C. Guenther, FAIA, LEED AP

1961: The Educational Apostolate in the St. Louis Arch Soffits

Hildreth Meière was working on the last of her sketches for the west arch soffit depicting the educational apostolate in St. Louis when she became ill and died in May 1961 due to the sudden onset of leukemia. The final two groups of figures and a building were completed by her assistant Nina Wheeler Blake, who had helped paint cartoons from Meière's sketches. The installation of the four arch soffits was completed posthumously, as was the installation of Meière's design for the south wall surrounding the rose window.

Meière created designs for the cathedral for almost two decades, starting in 1945. She described her works as "a labor of faith and love." The Cathedral Basilica of Saint Louis is truly blessed to feature nine of her magnificent designs, created at the height of her career, on such a grand scale.

Meière was an established liturgical artist at a time when religious institutions commissioned extensive, integral architectural decorations and highly skilled European craftsmen were available to fabricate and execute her designs.

Writing in 1956, Meière acknowledged, "It is perfectly possible that I will not live long enough to see all the areas completed." Sadly, her intuition was correct. Meière did not live to see the beauty of all of her mosaic designs for the south nave completed.

On January 19, 1961, Pope John XXIII created and proclaimed Joseph Elmer Ritter a cardinal. It was a moment of immense civic and ecclesiastical pride for St. Louis Catholics. The next day, John Fitzgerald Kennedy was inaugurated as the 35th president of the United States—the first Roman Catholic to hold that office.

On January 27, 1961, Pope John XXIII decreed that the Church of St. Louis, King of France (Old Cathedral) become a Basilica, known officially as the Basilica of St. Louis, King of France, recognizing the original cathedral's significance.

1962: South Wall

As Hildreth Meière contemplated the design of the south wall, surrounding the blue south rose window, she envisioned a "series of borders, and an all-over diaper pattern for the soffit and outer area of the south wall" along with repeating the Art Deco–style, gold Meandering Grapevine with smaller, tighter, more stylized tendrils and design motifs and colors she had employed for the north end wall surrounding the north red rose window.

Meière told Arno Heuduck at Ravenna Mosaics that the color tone she wanted for her design on the south wall was green, to complement the window's "outer purple-blue," which she thought was "terrific."

Meière never saw her design of the south wall completed, as the Byzantine-style glass mosaics were not installed before her death in May 1961. Fortunately, she had finished her sketches. Nina Wheeler Blake, her assistant, painted the full-scale cartoons, which allowed the mosaicists to fabricate Meière's designs, resulting in the south wall being completed posthumously in 1962.

The south wall surrounding rose window with Meandering Grapevine was commissioned by George John Maguolo, fabricated by Pühl & Wagner, and installed by Ravenna Mosaics.

South rose window mosaics designed by Hildreth Meière
Photograph by Serhii Chrucky © Serhii Chrucky I Esto

Maronite services at the cathedral on September 10, 1962
Westrich
Courtesy of Archdiocese of St. Louis Archives

Joseph E. Ritter ordained 19 men into the priesthood on April 9, 1962.
St. Louis Globe-Democrat Collection, from the collections of the St. Louis Mercantile Library, University of Missouri–St. Louis

1962: Historical Arch Soffits

With the pendentives and the south dome completed, Meière designed the four arch soffits, depicting the history of the Catholic Church in St. Louis.

The themes of the four arch soffits include the History of Spiritual Growth in St. Louis (south arch soffit), Educational Apostolate in St. Louis (west arch soffit), St. Vincent de Paul and His Followers (north arch soffit), and the Social Apostolate in St. Louis (east arch soffit). The arch soffits are made with the vibrant gold ground of Byzantine-style glass mosaic.

Hildreth Meière's design of History of the Catholic Church in St. Louis was also completed posthumously in 1962. She was commissioned by George John Maguolo. Meière's artistic collaborator was Nina Wheeler Blake. The Byzantine-style glass mosaics were fabricated by Pühl & Wagner of Berlin and installed by Ravenna Mosaics of St. Louis.

St. Louis was the first diocese west of the Mississippi River, established in 1826, and almost equal to the Louisiana Territory. Louis-Guillaume-Valentin DuBourg arrived in 1818, serving as the first bishop.

St. Louis was the site of the first American foundations of the Religious of the Sacred Heart, the Congregation of the Mission, the Brothers of the Christian Schools, the Sisters of St. Joseph, and the Ursulines. It was home of the second foundation of the Sisters of Loretto, the Daughters of Charity, the Visitation Sisters, the Jesuits, the Sisters of the Good Shepherd, and others. St. Louis became the first archdiocese of the American Midwest in 1847.

Other firsts include the first college (St. Mary's in Perryville) and the first university (Saint Louis University) chartered west of the Mississippi River, the first hospital (the Saint Louis Charity Hospital), and the first seminary (St. Mary's in Perryville).

Historical Arch (south arch soffit), November 1960

Courtesy of International Hildreth Meière Association

1962: Four Arch Soffits of Local History

Educational Apostolate in St. Louis (west arch soffit)

Symbol of Education—a lamp on open book upon cross; DuBourg High School; Sisters of Loretto at the foot of the cross; School Sisters of Notre Dame; Ursuline Nuns of the Roman Union; Saint Louis University; Society of Mary (Saints Peter and Paul's, Chaminade, McBride, St. Mary's, Vianney); Brothers of the Christian Schools (Christian Brothers College—CBC)

History of Spiritual Growth in St. Louis (south arch soffit)

The Common Seal of the City of St. Louis; First Mass, December 8, 1698, on west bank of Mississippi River on site of the future St. Louis; first baptism, early 1766, of Marie Deschamps by Father Meurin in a tent for lack of a church; Old Spanish Church, second log church, built 1776, dedicated June 24, 1776; Old Cathedral—the Basilica of St. Louis, King of France, built 1831–34

St. Vincent de Paul and Followers (north arch soffit)

The Miraculous Medal; Ozanam Shelter (Home for Men); four St. Louis charitable leaders: Dr. Moses Linton, old St. Louis Medical College; Frederick Ozanam, founder of St. Vincent de Paul Society; Bryan Mullanphy, lay apostle and philanthropist; Bishop John Timon, early Vincentian missionary; Kenrick Seminary, built 1913–15; Very Reverend Felix de Andreis; Joseph Rosati, second bishop of St. Louis (1827–43); St. Vincent de Paul, founder, Congregation of the Missions

Social Apostolate (east arch soffit)

Caritas; Glennon Memorial Hospital; Sisters of Mercy; Sisters of St. Mary; Franciscan Sisters; Alexian Brothers; Little Sisters of the Poor; Sisters of St. Joseph; Sisters of the Good Shepherd; Sisters of the Most Precious Blood

Photographs courtesy of International Hildreth Meière Association

Arch of the Last Judgment, 1962
John (Jan Henryk) de Rosen (1891–1982), artist
Photograph by Serhii Chrucky © Serhii Chrucky I Esto

John (Jan Henryk) de Rosen (1891–1982)
Photograph by Jan Neuman (1900–41)
Courtesy of Narodowe Archiwum

Scaffolding erected for interior mosaic work in 1963
Photographer Peter Ferman, May 31, 1963
Courtesy of Archdiocese of St. Louis Archives

1963: Arch of the Last Judgment

Jan (later John) Henryk de Rosen (1891–1982) was a Polish artist of murals and mosaics. Having served in World War I in various capacities, achieving the rank of captain in the Polish army, and earning military honors, de Rosen, a hero in the struggle for Polish independence, also served as a diplomat for Poland.

He moved to the United States in 1939, where he completed large-scale commissions for churches and other institutions, and he became a research professor of liturgical arts at The Catholic University of America in Washington, DC.

John de Rosen designed the Arch of the Last Judgment. His process involved making a three-dimensional cloth model to shape and draw the forms for the sketches and full-size cartoon in full color. A reverse tracing was then made and cut into jigsaw puzzle pieces, with color-matched glass tesserae glued to each piece. These smaller panels were then reassembled on the cathedral surface, placed face forward into wet mortar, with the tesserae tapped in at different angles to catch the light and sparkle. Later, the paper was peeled off to reveal the mosaics, which were then cleaned and grouted.

The Arch of the Last Judgment represents the last judgment with Christ presiding as judge. He is flanked by two angels—one holding a book of judgment, the other a scepter representing Christ's authority. At the left, three of the dead rise from their tombs. St. Peter stands at the gates of paradise, with St. Dismas and Mary, Mother of Mercy, above. At the right, St. John the Baptist offers his head as sacrifice, with St. Michael the Archangel and St. Odilo, "the shepherd or light of the dying," with the group of the doomed, nameless and faceless, in hell represented by ice and snow—very cold for the lack of love.

The Arch of the Last Judgment mosaics were installed by Paul Heuduck, chairman and owner of the Ravenna Company, and his son, Arno Heuduck, who completed the commission in 1963.

John de Rosen developing his design with cloth model and cartoon of the Arch of the Last Judgment

Courtesy of *Globe-Democrat Sunday Magazine*, October 14, 1963

Arch of the Last Judgment and south pendentives of the central dome

Photograph by Serhii Chrucky © Serhii Chrucky I Esto

1963: Main Dome South Pendentives

Professor August Oetken designed the two south pendentives of the central dome in 1924. They were fabricated at the same time as the Angel of the New Law (northwest) pendentive (installed 1925) and the Angel of the Old Law (northeast) pendentive (installed 1925) in an effort to maximize efficiency and keep costs down. The southeast and southwest pendentive mosaics were kept in storage in the basement of the Cathedral of Saint Louis after fabrication.

They were refabricated, as the paper backup had deteriorated after 38 years in storage. The southeast pendentive and the southwest pendentive were installed in 1963, at the same time as the Arch of the Last Judgment.

The southeast pendentive, central dome, represents secular authority, symbolized by the scepter and the crown.
OMNUS ANIMA PROTESTATIBUS SUBLIMIORIBUS SUBDITA EST (Every individual is subject to higher powers.)
Photograph by Sam Fentress, © SAM FENTRESS PHOTOGRAPHY

1963: Exterior Restoration and Interior Mosaics

For the second time in 12 years, the facade of the Cathedral of Saint Louis was covered in scaffolding, allowing various firms to inspect the building walls more carefully before submitting bids to waterproof where necessary. The work was considered "normal maintenance" by Western Waterproofing Company, Inc., who tuck-pointed and waterproofed the cathedral in 1951. They noted that in a building the size of the cathedral "a lot of movement takes place seasonally that does not happen in smaller buildings" due in part to the towers adjoining the walls and arches.

Extensive repair and remodeling work at the Cathedral of Saint Louis began in 1963, with exterior scaffolding in place for about seven weeks, to allow for bidding and completion of the necessary work.

Inside the huge cathedral, scaffolding was erected over the central nave area in order to permit further work on the mosaic art on the Arch of the Last Judgment and two pendentives adjoining it.

On Friday November 22, 1963, John F. Kennedy, the 35th president of the United States, was assassinated while riding in a presidential motorcade through Dealey Plaza in Dallas, Texas.

On Monday November 25, 1963, the Cathedral of Saint Louis was packed with mourners gathered for a Requiem Mass for President John F. Kennedy on the same day as his funeral in Washington, DC.

The cathedral is covered in scaffolding during restoration of exterior granite (May 24, 1963).

Photograph by Peter Ferman. Courtesy of Archdiocese of St. Louis Archives

John Fitzgerald Kennedy

35th president of the United States

Born May 29, 1917

Inaugurated January 20, 1961

Died November 22, 1963

Scaffolding was erected over the central nave area for mosaic art installation (1963).

Photographer: Jack J. Zehrt. Courtesy of Archdiocese of St. Louis Archives

Cardinal Ritter ordained 24 men from Kenrick Seminary to the priesthood, along with eight other members of religious orders, March 14, 1964.

St. Louis Globe-Democrat Collection, from the collections of the St. Louis Mercantile Library, University of Missouri–St. Louis

Cardinal Ritter saying Mass facing the congregation for the first time, April 27, 1964

St. Louis Globe-Democrat Collection, from the collections of the St. Louis Mercantile Library, University of Missouri–St. Louis

Baldacchino cleaning, March 1964

Photographer: Jack J. Zehrt

Globe-Democrat Sunday Magazine, March 1, 1964

Courtesy of Archdiocese of St. Louis Archives

1964: Vatican II and a New Altar

The reform of the Roman Rite of Mass that was carried out after the Second Vatican Council (October 1, 1962–December 8, 1965) significantly altered the shape of Catholic worship, including the construction of new freestanding altars, built closer to the people. The *versus populum* (Latin for "toward the people") celebration was adopted throughout the Latin Church, becoming the prevailing practice during Mass for the celebrant to stand behind the altar facing the congregation.

Another significant change that emerged from the Vatican II council was the reform of the liturgy, including the use of vernacular language in Catholic worship to make the liturgy more accessible and understandable to contemporary worshippers, with priests celebrating the Mass in their respective languages, such as English, Spanish, or French.

The 57-foot-high, ornate marble baldacchino underwent its annual cleaning, with the help of steeple jacks operating from bosun's chairs suspended on steel anchors anchored into the dome of the cathedral. Beginning in 1952, the work was done by Frank Sager & Son, 7320 Eugene Avenue, with refinements over time, including the use of a two-way radio to communicate between the workmen attaching the steel cables to the outer dome structure and those below.

As much as a quarter of an inch of dust was cleaned from the top of the baldacchino. The installation of additional mosaics and an air-conditioning system contributed to this dust. Workmen washing the statues, mosaics, and marble surfaces worked in their bare feet so as to not grind dirt into the highly polished surfaces. The cleaned surfaces were then waxed. The operation took two to two-and-one-half working days by a crew of three or four. The dome of the baldacchino is supported by 10 marble columns, each 20 feet in height, 2 feet in diameter, and weighing 6 tons each.

Following Vatican II, on March 19, 1964, Cardinal Ritter established the Archdiocesan Commission on Ecumenism. On August 24, Ritter made history at the old Kiel Auditorium when he celebrated the world's first authorized Mass in English.

1965: Central Dome

In February 1962, Bishop Gottwald announced that the original design for the main central dome prepared by Hildreth Meière was no longer going forward after her untimely death in May 1961. John de Rosen was selected to create a new design for the central dome, subject to approval. De Rosen, a well-known artist, had designed the mosaics for the National Shrine of the Immaculate Conception in Washington, DC.

By July 1964, work on the central dome was underway, with scaffolding erected in two weeks. The central dome's spherical surface—11,000 square feet, with the top of the dome 143 feet above the floor—is one of the largest mosaic domes in the world. The mosaic installation began in August 1964 and took nine months.

The great dome had 16 of the 32 windows bricked in and was thoroughly scrubbed before the mosaics were applied. De Rosen's design, depicting scenes in the glorification of the Holy Trinity, suggested links between the revelation of the Old and New Testaments. It is composed of four sections of mosaics portraying various themes, including the prophet Elijah being carried into heaven, the vision of the prophet Ezekiel, Our Lady of the Apocalypse, and the Holy Trinity.

The dome was covered with a "brown-coat" of mortar about three-fourths of an inch thick with the mosaics embedded into this coating, thus becoming part of the building itself.

Paul Heuduck (1882–1972) and Arno Heuduck (1917–89), father and son, of Ravenna Mosaics, installed the mosaic design by De Rosen, who had been in St. Louis for three years working on various mosaic designs.

Central dome mosaics being completed in spring, 1965

Photograph by Richard Finke. Courtesy of Archdiocese of St. Louis Archives

Central dome (1965–66)

John (Jan Henryk) de Rosen (1891–1982), artist

Photograph by John C. Guenther, FAIA, LEED AP

Main dome partial model, 1950s

Arno Heuduck (1917–89) and Paul Heuduck (1882–1972)

Courtesy of Saint Louis University Libraries Special Collection

Children view the 1965 demolition of the Cathedral School of 1916 to clear the site for the new Cathedral School.

Photograph by Richard Finke. Courtesy of Archdiocese of St. Louis Archives

Chancery Building (1961), Cathedral School (1966), and Cathedral of Saint Louis

Photograph by Richard Finke. Courtesy of Archdiocese of St. Louis Archives

1966: New Cathedral School

The Cathedral School was founded and built in 1916, following the founding of the parish in 1896. The Sisters of the Sacred Heart staffed the school for the first five years. The Sisters of St. Joseph, Carondelet, staffed the school from 1921 until May 2017, when it closed.

The St. Louis cathedral parish built a convent for the Sisters of St. Joseph to the west of the parish school on Maryland Avenue. The two-story brick convent accommodated nine sisters and contained 15 rooms, including a chapel, dining room, kitchen, parlors, community room, and full basement. Gerald T. Lawlor built the $54,000 convent in 1960.

The new school to serve 200 students was first announced in the *St. Louis Review* in September 1964. Designed by Murphy & Mackey, architects, the new Cathedral School was composed of a school wing with 10 classrooms, a library, administrative offices, a teachers' lounge, a health room, and an auditorium wing with a cafeteria on the ground floor, and an auditorium on the second floor that could seat 500 for diocesan-wide meetings and assemblies, and could also be used as a gymnasium. Gray brick, and some stone trim, was selected to harmonize with the granite of the cathedral.

Construction for the two-year project began on November 1, 1964, with the razing of the old gymnasium and auditorium, which was to be the site of the new classroom building. After the new classrooms were finished, the new gymnasium-auditorium was built on the site of the old classroom building.

The new Cathedral School for the St. Louis cathedral parish was completed in 1966 and was to have been dedicated by Cardinal Ritter on Sunday September 18, 1966. The dedication was postponed due to death of Father Aloysius J. Boland, cathedral assistant, that week.

East sanctuary wall, which depicts the Passover, installed in 1967, designed by Professor August Oetken (1868–1951) in 1924

Photograph by Sam Fentress, © SAM FENTRESS PHOTOGRAPHY

West sanctuary wall, which depicts the Last Supper, installed in 1967, designed by Professor August Oetken (1868–1951) in 1924

Photograph by Sam Fentress, © SAM FENTRESS PHOTOGRAPHY

1967: Sanctuary Mosaics

The mosaics depicting the Passover (the Seder—Old Testament prototype of the Eucharist) and the Last Supper (the fulfillment of the Passover, at which Christ instituted the Eucharist) in the gallery level of the east and west sanctuary walls were installed in 1967. They were both designed by Professor August Oetken in 1924.

Robert Harmon (1903–90) designed the west arch soffit above the Last Supper mosaic. It was installed in 1947. It features the Nativity scene at Bethlehem, the Miracle of Cana, and a large cross at the center, surrounded by the sun, moon, stars, and rain.

In May 1967, Western Waterproofing Company, Inc. prepared its estimate and approach to the restoration of miscellaneous masonry joints and the restoration of joints and cracks in the movement of the east, north, west, and the base of the south elevations. They caulked the joints and cracks in movement in the top joints of the parapet walls. They also provided miscellaneous tuck-pointing in masonry joints, removing loose and disintegrated mortar, cleaning the joints, and re-pointing them with nonshrinking Dilato mortar, matching the existing mortar color.

1967: The Passing of Cardinal Ritter

Joseph Cardinal Elmer Ritter died at 74 on Saturday morning, June 10, 1967, after suffering two heart attacks, first on Monday June 5, and then on Wednesday June 7. He received the last rites after being admitted to DePaul Hospital. Beginning on Wednesday June 7, a vigil was kept by high archdiocesan officers and members of Cardinal Ritter's family, including his sister, a nun, Sister M. Catherine Ritter of the Sisters of Charity of Nazareth in Bardstown, Kentucky.

Born in New Albany, Indiana, on July 20, 1892, he was ordained in 1917 and celebrated the 50th anniversary of his ordination on April 30, 1967, with a Mass of Thanksgiving at the Cathedral of Saint Louis. He was looking forward to his 75th birthday in June 1967.

Cardinal Ritter became archbishop of the St. Louis Diocese in 1946, following the death of Cardinal John J. Glennon. He received his scarlet cap and robe of a cardinal from Pope John XXIII in 1960. He was regarded as the chief American spokesman at the Second Vatican Council.

Cardinal Ritter's funeral was held on Thursday June 15, 1967, with the Cathedral of Saint Louis filled to capacity. Hundreds of Catholic prelates, priests, and nuns, as well as representatives of other faiths and members of the laity, came to attend and participate in the services for Cardinal Ritter, who had administered the affairs of the Archdiocese of St. Louis for 21 years. He was buried in Calvary Cemetery.

Requiem Mass for Joseph Cardinal Ritter, June 15, 1967

St. Louis Globe-Democrat Collection, from the collections of the St. Louis Mercantile Library, University of Missouri–St. Louis

Funeral for Joseph Cardinal Ritter, June 15, 1967

St. Louis Globe-Democrat Collection, from the collections of the St. Louis Mercantile Library, University of Missouri–St. Louis

Mass for Martin Luther King, Jr., April 6, 1968

John J. Carberry, main celebrant of a special Mass for Martin Luther King, Jr. at the Cathedral of Saint Louis. Photograph by Richard Finke. Courtesy of Archdiocese of St. Louis Archives

Martin Luther King, Jr. (1929–68)

1968: Memorial Mass for Dr. Martin Luther King, Jr.

Bishop John J. Carberry (1904–98) was named archbishop of St. Louis on February 21, 1968, by Pope Paul VI. He was installed as the fifth archbishop of St. Louis on March 25, 1968. Arriving in turbulent days of social upheaval, Carberry served as archbishop of St. Louis from 1968 to 1979 and was a strong advocate for ecumenicism and racial equality. Carberry was elevated to cardinal on April 28, 1969, by Pope Paul VI.

Dr. Martin Luther King, Jr. (1929–68) was an American Baptist minister, activist, Nobel Peace Prize laureate, and one of the most prominent leaders in the Civil Rights Movement from 1955 until his assassination in Memphis, Tennessee, where he was speaking in support of the black sanitation workers, represented by the American Federation of State, County and Municipal Employees (AFSCME) Local 1733, who were on strike for higher wages and better treatment. King was fatally shot by James Earl Ray at 6:01 p.m. on Thursday April 4, 1968, as he stood on the Lorraine Motel's second-floor balcony.

On Saturday April 6, 1968, Archbishop Carberry was the main celebrant of a special memorial Mass for Dr. King at the Cathedral of Saint Louis, attended by 2,000, and open to people of all faiths.

Archbishop Carberry said the work of Dr. King would continue. "No sniper's bullet can stop his work, for it is founded upon the moral law and the solid basis of justice for all."

Father Paul Gopaul, an Edmundite father and a member of the Archdiocesan Commission on Human Rights, delivered a powerful sermon to "my fellow mourners" and called Dr. King a "true man of God, prophet with honor and herald of better things to come."

In addition to Archbishop Carberry and Father Gopaul, Mass celebrants included Msgr. Thomas F. Durkin, Msgr. Mark Ebner, Msgr. Patrick J. Molloy, Father Francis M. Doyle, Father Edward J. O'Donnell, Father John Schocklee, and Father Arthur M. Peet.

1968: Memorial March for Dr. Martin Luther King, Jr.

A memorial march for Dr. Martin Luther King, Jr. was held in St. Louis on Sunday, April 7, 1968. An estimated 2,000 people gathered at the Gateway Arch grounds one half hour before the march was to begin. The Reverend Vinton A. Anderson and the Reverend Cleophus Robinson spoke at the tribute to Dr. King. After taps were played, at 1:33 p.m. the marchers left the Gateway Arch grounds and followed an empty hearse down Washington Avenue. Two-and-a-half hours later, 30,000 had gathered in Forest Park for the conclusion of the march.

On Monday evening, April 8, 1968, hundreds of St. Louisans left by bus for Atlanta to attend Dr. King's funeral Tuesday morning.

Those from St. Louis attending Dr. King's funeral on Tuesday April 9, 1968, included Father Paul Gopaul; Father Francis M. Doyle; Father Edward J. O'Donnell; Louis McKinnie and Richard Childress of the Archdiocesan Commission on Human Rights; Sister Peter Claver, a Sister of St. Mary; Sister Eustelle Marie, principal of Holy Rosary; Father Jerome Brazkowski, SVD, pastor of St. Nicholas Parish; Father Anthony Siebert, associate pastor of Most Holy Rosary Parish; and James Smith, a parishioner of the parish.

Marchers followed an empty hearse down Washington Avenue to Forest Park.

Two thousand people gathered at the Gateway Arch grounds one half hour before the march, growing to 7,000 by the 1:30 p.m. start of the eight-mile march to Forest Park.

Marchers on Washington Avenue

All photographs on this page are by Richard Finke. Courtesy of Archdiocese of St. Louis Archives

1968: New Marble Altar

Workmen set in place a new, permanent marble altar in the sanctuary of the Cathedral of Saint Louis, replacing the temporary wooden altar that had been in use for some time. The altar was constructed in Italy and shipped here. It was used at the Christmas midnight Mass.

The new marble altar faced the worshipers in accordance with the liturgical changes called for by Vatican II in the Mass several years earlier, so the priest could face the people.

The altar was a gift of Cardinal John J. Carberry, made possible by a personal legacy.

On December 24, 1968, Cardinal Carberry consecrated this altar of Sacrifice in the Cathedral of Saint Louis and placed in it the relics of the Saints Clement, Aurelius, Liberatus, martyrs, and of Pope St. Pius X.

It was used for the first time at Christmas Eve midnight Mass on December 25, 1968.

The altar features a pair of peacocks, symbols of immortality, and a large jeweled mosaic cross in the center section.

It was removed and relocated to the basement chapel of the Cathedral of Saint Louis when a new altar was designed and installed in 1986.

Joseph Murphy, FAIA, of Murphy & Mackey Architects, prepared studies for the relocation of the altar to beneath the central dome, rearranging the sanctuary and the pews. These ideas were not pursued.

New altar, 1968. Courtesy of Cathedral Basilica of Saint Louis Archives

New altar at the Cathedral of Saint Louis being assembled December 12, 1968. Photographs by Richard Finke

Courtesy of Archdiocese of St. Louis Archives

Wooden altar in use for several years, facing worshipers in accordance with the liturgical changes called for by Vatican II. Photograph by Richard Finke

Courtesy of Archdiocese of St. Louis Archives

Cardinal Wojtyła visits the Old Cathedral.

On September 26, 1969, Karol Cardinal Wojtyła, archbishop of Krakow, Poland, made a visit to the Old Cathedral. Nine years later, he became Pope John Paul II, succeeding Pope John Paul I.

Photograph by Richard Finke. Courtesy of Archdiocese of St. Louis Archives

Rt. Rev. Joseph Rosati, CM (1789–1843)

First bishop of St. Louis (1827–43)

Courtesy of the Cathedral Basilica of Saint Louis Archives

Bishop Joseph Rosati crypt beneath sanctuary of the Old Cathedral

Photograph by John C. Guenther, FAIA, LEED AP

1970: Bishop Rosati's Final Resting Place

In 1970, Cardinal John Carberry granted the request of Auxiliary Bishop Joseph McNicholas (1923–83), rector at the Old Cathedral, to move Bishop Joseph Rosati (1789–1843) to his final resting place at the cathedral that he built: the Basilica of St. Louis, King of France. His tomb sits beneath the sanctuary of the church.

The body of Bishop Rosati was buried beneath the main altar of the historic Old Cathedral at a Mass at 5:30 p.m. on Saturday May 23, 1970. Concelebrants of the Mass were Bishop McNicholas and Father James A. Fischer, provincial of the Western Province of the Vincentian Fathers, the religious order to which Bishop Rosati belonged. The Mass was offered for him and other deceased priests, religious and laymen who worked with Rosati to build the Cathedral of St. Louis (Old Cathedral).

Rosati had served as bishop (1827–43), during which time he planned and brought to completion the construction of the Old Cathedral, dedicating it in 1834.

Rosati died in Rome in 1843 and was buried there until 1954, when his body was brought back to St. Louis and solemnly reinterred in a crypt in the new Cathedral of Saint Louis.

The transfer of the body was arranged because of Bishop Rosati's close association with the Old Cathedral and in conjunction with the 200th anniversary of the Old Cathedral parish being observed in 1970.

According to Auxiliary Bishop Joseph A. McNicholas, then pastor of the Basilica of St. Louis, King of France (Old Cathedral): "The thousands of visitors to the Old Cathedral each year express a great interest in the history of the Old Cathedral and it is most fitting that the mortal remains of its builder be buried beneath the altar."

1972–76: Official St. Louis Landmark

Paul J. Heuduck died at the age of 90 on September 8, 1972. He was a master craftsman of the art of glass tesserae mosaics, having begun working in that medium at the age of 14. Heuduck came to St. Louis from Berlin to help establish Ravenna Mosaic, Inc., founded by Emil Frei, Sr. in 1923, for the purpose of installing the mosaics for the Cathedral of Saint Louis, where Heuduck spent 42 years completing most of the elaborate mosaics.

Heuduck became the owner of the Ravenna Company in 1937. He climbed the scaffolding more than 100 feet above the cathedral floor to install the mosaics until he was in his mid-60s. He retired from the business at age 89. Arno Heuduck, Paul's son and vice president of Ravenna Mosaic Company, carried on the work, which was more than 90 percent complete at the time, after his father's retirement.

In 1974, Paul Heuduck moved Ravenna Mosaic Company from 5205 South Grand Boulevard to an outbuilding at his country home in Fredericktown, Missouri.

In October 1973, the Cathedral Basilica of Saint Louis was honored as an official Landmark of the City of St. Louis. Architect Verner I. Burks, chairman, Landmarks and Urban Design Commission, City of St. Louis, wrote to Cardinal John J. Carberry with the good news on October 4, 1973.

Our Lady of Perpetual Help Shrine was a gift to the cathedral by Cardinal Carberry in memory of his parents, James J. and Mary E. Carberry, and his deceased brothers and sisters. The marble mosaic shrine of Our Lady of Perpetual Help is located north of and adjacent to the All Saints Chapel and forms a focal point when viewed from the Chapel of Our Lady. The 1976 design was by Joseph Dennis Murphy, FAIA (1907–95), of Murphy, Downey, Wofford & Richman.

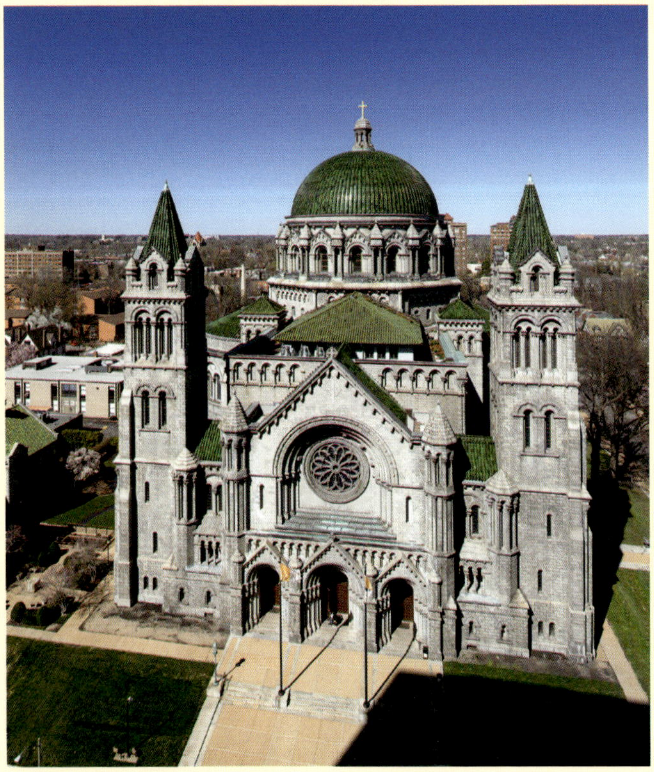

The Cathedral Basilica of Saint Louis was honored as an official Landmark of the City of St. Louis, October 4, 1973.

Photograph by Serhii Chrucky © Serhii Chrucky I Esto

Our Lady of Perpetual Help Shrine. Designed by Joseph Murphy, FAIA. Arno Heuduck, Ravenna Mosaic Company

Photograph by Richard Finke, 1976. Courtesy of Archdiocese of St. Louis Archives

Memorial Mass for Pope Paul VI

Three auxiliary bishops and 22 priests concelebrate a memorial Mass for Pope Paul VI with 1,500 in attendance in the Cathedral of Saint Louis, August 11, 1978. Photograph by Paul Ockrassa. From the collections of the St. Louis Mercantile Library, University of Missouri–St. Louis

1978: Memorial Mass for Pope Paul VI

On August 6, 1978, Pope Paul VI suffered a massive heart attack after receiving communion and died in Castel Gandolfo.

Pope Paul VI (1897–1978) was eulogized as "one of the greatest individuals of this entire century" at a memorial Mass on Friday evening, August 11, 1978, at the Cathedral of Saint Louis.

Bishop John N. Wurm gave the homily, noting that "He led the world and the bark of Peter through troubled times," and that the Pope was a "sign of contradiction" in this era just as Jesus Christ was in His time.

The main celebrants were St. Louis Auxiliary Bishops Wurm, George J. Gottwald, and Charles V. Koester, who along with 22 priests concelebrated a memorial Mass for Pope Paul VI with 1,600 in attendance in the Cathedral of Saint Louis.

Mayor Jim Conway and former Mayor John H. Poelker read scripture passages.

A long procession consisting of Catholic clergy, lay Catholic groups, Protestant clergy, the Knights of Columbus honor guard, the Knights and Ladies of the Holy Sepulcher, and the Knights of Malta made its way through the nave of the cathedral, which Pope Paul VI had visited in 1951 when he was an assistant secretary of state at the Vatican.

In 1978, Cardinal John Carberry, archbishop of St. Louis (1968–79) transferred all buildings and property of Old St. Ferdinand to the Friends of Old St. Ferdinand, Inc.—a group established in 1958 to maintain and preserve the historic structures after Old St. Ferdinand ceased to be a parish in 1955. All four buildings were included on the National Register of Historic Places in 1979 as the St. Ferdinand's Shrine Historic District. The Archdiocese of St. Louis designated the historic complex as a shrine to St. Rose Philippine Duchesne upon her canonization in 1988.

The cathedral architectural features and recesses offered a good perch to view the processional, March 26, 1980.

St. Louis Globe-Democrat Collection, from the collections of the St. Louis Mercantile Library, University of Missouri–St. Louis

Rev. Dennis Delaney and Robert Clark hung the Archbishop May Coat of Arms at the New Cathedral on March 22, 1980. Photograph by Richard Finke. Courtesy of Archdiocese of St. Louis Archives

1980: Archbishop May

Having turned 75 and in accordance with Code of Canon Law, Cardinal John J. Carberry submitted his resignation to Pope John Paul II. Carberry lived in retirement until his death on June 17, 1998, at the age of 93.

Carberry's successor, John Lawrence May, was installed as the sixth archbishop of St. Louis on March 26, 1980, with more than 2,000 people in attendance.

After studies at Saint Mary of the Lake Seminary in Mundelein, Illinois, May was ordained a priest on May 3, 1947.

May was ordained auxiliary bishop of Chicago on August 24, 1967. He became archbishop of Mobile, Alabama, on December 10, 1969. May was installed as archbishop of the Archdiocese of St. Louis on March 25, 1980. From 1983 until 1989 May served as vice president and then as president of the United States Conference of Catholic Bishops.

Archbishop May was a strong advocate of dialogue between Christians of all denominations, desegregation of public schools, and improved race relations. As archbishop, he ordained the first African American auxiliary bishop of St. Louis, J. Terry Steib, SVD, a native of Vacherie, Louisiana.

John Lawrence May (1922–94)

Courtesy of Archdiocese of St. Louis Archives

May named a layperson as the archdiocese's first chief financial officer, and he appointed the first woman superintendent of Catholic schools.

Throughout the 1980s, Archbishop May led calls for increasing aid to the poor and homeless, including an expansion of Catholic Charities' programs to assist those in need.

Archbishop May fostered the cause of Blessed Philippine Duchesne (canonized on July 3, 1988) and the completion of the cathedral.

He served the Archdiocese of St. Louis until 1992.

1980: Reading Is Fundamental

The Cathedral School, founded and first built in 1916, following the founding of the parish in 1896, and later rebuilt as a modern structure in 1966, continued its important mission of educating the youth of the area in its prekindergarten to eight grade classes, with the Sisters of St. Joseph, Carondelet, staffing the school from 1921 onward.

In 1980, the Reading Is Fundamental (RIF) program was implemented at the Cathedral School—the first in an archdiocesan school. Of note, KMOX-TV's Julius Hunter, author of a popular children's alphabet book, was invited to kick off the Reading Is Fundamental (RIF) program on October 24, 1980.

As one who is dedicated to lifelong learning, education, and teaching, Julius Hunter recalled learning to read at an early age with the help of Van, his older brother, by reading the St. Louis telephone directory and the labels of food products from a local grocery store. It was fitting for Hunter to work with the classes at the Cathedral School to instill in those children a love for reading.

Julius Hunter's career included time as a grade school teacher, a copywriter for TV commercials, the director of a student outreach program called "Education in Action" at Washington University, and a pioneer for African American broadcast journalists. He worked as a reporter, weekend anchor, and weekend news director at NBC affiliate KSDK, eventually taking on expanded reporter and anchoring duties at CBS affiliate KMOX-TV and becoming the first African American to anchor a prime-time newscast in St. Louis, covering local, regional, national, and international news.

Hunter's remarkable broadcast, print, and public service career spanned four decades, during which he interviewed six sitting US presidents and innumerable local and nationally known politicians and celebrities. Hunter has authored numerous books, including the illustrated histories of Westmoreland and Portland Places and Kingsbury Place, a book on St. Louis trivia, and a college textbook on broadcast news.

In 1978, Hunter broadcast live reports from Rome on the deaths of Paul VI and John Paul I respectively, and he traveled with Pope John Paul II on three occasions.

Sister Monica Marie and first grader Jacques Woodson review a lesson.

Jacques is the son of Abe Woodson (1934–2014), football player for the St. Louis Cardinals (1965–66 season).

Photograph by Richard C. Finke. Courtesy of Archdiocese of St. Louis Archives

Reading anchorman, 1980

KMOX-TV's Julius Hunter, author of a children's book, anchors a reading session at the St. Louis Cathedral Parish School. Hunter was invited there to kick off the Reading Is Fundamental (RIF) program. RIF is designed to motivate children toward a love for reading.

Photograph by Richard C. Finke. Courtesy of Archdiocese of St. Louis Archives

Cathedral covered in scaffolding during the restoration of exterior granite for four years, July 29, 1980

St. Louis Globe-Democrat Collection, from the collections of the St. Louis Mercantile Library, University of Missouri–St. Louis

1980–85: A "More Than Routine" Restoration

A "more than routine" restoration of the exterior of the Cathedral of Saint Louis began in 1980, requiring five years and an undetermined budget, reported Monsignor Rowland E. Gannon, pastor of the cathedral parish. He noted, "It was a question of having a pockmarked building or maintaining it as it should be. There was no choice." There was serious "deterioration of stone" resulting from the weather, pollution, and the type of granite used in the structure.

In previous years, routine tuck-pointing was undertaken. In 1978, a study was commissioned that determined the need for a major repair project. Simpson Gumpertz & Heger of Cambridge, Massachusetts, attributed the deterioration to the freeze-thaw cycle of St. Louis winters, automobile pollution, and water seepage into the porous Concord, New Hampshire, granite of the building.

The restoration was done in sections, beginning with west porch repairs costing $30,000. Tuck-pointers next worked on the facade, followed by the front towers. Work also included installation of exterior gutters to replace the internal drain system and improvements to the roof and flashing. Horizontal and vertical mortar joints were raked, allowed to dry, and re-pointed. Some granite was replaced due to severe fracturing from the freeze-thaw cycles. The exterior repairs to the west tower were undertaken to correct a structural defect discovered where some exterior stones had pulled away from the building. Albert Alper, structural engineer of Alper Associates, Inc., recommended that four 12-foot-long stainless steel rods with stainless steel plates be installed within the west tower corners to address internal forces opening the corners. Wood louvers in the stone towers were also repaired and repainted.

Emil Frei, Inc. replaced broken and cracked pieces of art glass windows and recaulked and repainted window frames.

Joseph D. Murphy, FAIA, of Murphy & Mackey, and later Murphy, Downey, Wofford & Richman, architects of St. Louis, served as the official architect of the cathedral. They oversaw the major seven-year exterior renovation project to correct the moisture problem disintegrating the granite walls and roof. Murphy also designed the shrine of Our Lady of Perpetual Help and the Cathedral School, with Eugene J. Mackey, Jr., FAIA.

Cathedral covered in scaffolding during restoration of exterior granite

Photograph by Richard C. Finke. Courtesy of Archdiocese of St. Louis Archives

East transept reroofing with new membrane and nailers, 1984

Photograph by Richard C. Finke. Courtesy of Archdiocese of St. Louis Archives

1980–85: Transept Roofs

G. T. Lawlor Construction Co. was selected for the restoration project. Robert Downey served as project architect for the whole of the exterior work.

The primary concern was with the two transepts, east and west, where the new interior mosaics were to be installed. The exterior work on these vital areas had to be done before the mosaics could be installed in order to ensure their safety.

Once the roof tiles were removed over the half domes of the transepts, it was discovered that the lightweight concrete had deteriorated. It was replaced over the structural concrete half dome. Roof tiles were reinstalled, and some cracked or damaged roof tiles were replaced. They were installed over a new Derbigum roof membrane and wood nailers.

Stone walls were properly capped with copper, and the two-foot-wide hidden copper gutter was repaired with a lead-coated copper edge cap.

East transept reroofing with new membrane and wood nailers, 1984

Photograph by Richard C. Finke. Courtesy of Archdiocese of St. Louis Archives

East transept reroofing with tile roof removed, 1984

Photograph by Richard C. Finke. Courtesy of Archdiocese of St. Louis Archives

East transept reroofing with new tile roof, 1984

Photograph by Richard C. Finke. Courtesy of Archdiocese of St. Louis Archives

East transept mosaic-painting water damage, 1984
Photograph by Richard C. Finke
Courtesy of Archdiocese of St. Louis Archives

Max Starkloff heads up the new permanent ramp of the cathedral, 1982.
Photograph by Richard C. Finke
Courtesy of Archdiocese of St. Louis Archives

1982: Transept Half Domes Assessment

Architect Joseph D. Murphy, FAIA prepared a study in 1981 regarding the condition of the al secco mosaic-paintings of the east and west half-dome transepts of the cathedral and related arch soffits. Restoration was not recommended, with new glass tesserae mosaic designs being preferred.

In 1982, Mary Reardon, artist, of Hingham, Massachusetts, received the commission to design the mosaics for the east transept vault—the Resurrection (1984)—and the west transept vault—the Pentecost (1986)—from Archbishop John L. May.

Mother Teresa (August 26, 1910–September 5, 1997) visited the New Cathedral on June 8, 1982, and addressed those gathered there.

In 1982, a new permanent ramp was installed on the west side of the cathedral adjacent to a parking lot to provide an accessible entrance. Max Starkloff (1937–2010) was a member of the St. Louis Cathedral Parish. He sought to make the world more accessible for the disabled, and founded Paraquad in 1970—an organization that seeks to develop the community to include all disabled persons.

Jan Henryk de Rosen, 91, died August 22, 1982. His design for the mosaics of the central dome was the largest in the world at 14,000 square feet.

Mother Teresa visited the New Cathedral on June 8, 1982, and addressed those gathered there.

Photograph by Richard C. Finke

Courtesy of Archdiocese of St. Louis Archives

1983: New Designs for the East Transept

Mary Reardon's first commission for the Cathedral of Saint Louis was to design the mosaics for the east transept—the Resurrection. The committee in charge asked that the concept reflect the influence of theology on the multiple appearances of the Risen Christ in a more contemporary style. The color tone is lighter and brighter to suggest the transfiguring glory of the Risen Christ. Reardon developed and refined the design in 1982.

"Most important water color sketch painted in St. Louis Cathedral, 3/22/1982. Approved on spot by Archbishop May," as noted by Mary Reardon, artist

Courtesy of Cathedral Basilica of Saint Louis Archives

Meeting at Ravenna Mosaic, Inc., Fredericktown, Missouri, April 15, 1983

Left to right: G. T. Lawlor; Arno Heuduck; Joseph Murphy, FAIA; Msgr. Rowland Gannon; Verner Burks, FAIA; Maurice McNamee, SJ; Rev. John Gaydos; Mrs. Heuduck; Archbishop May; Mary Reardon

Courtesy of Cathedral Basilica of Saint Louis Archives

Preliminary sketch of Arch of Resurrection soffit, March 22, 1982

Mary Reardon, artist, March 1982

Courtesy of Cathedral Basilica of Saint Louis Archives

Mosaic design from cartoon with Arno Heuduck

Photograph by Richard C. Finke. Courtesy of Cathedral Basilica of Saint Louis Archives

Mosaic for hand, east transept dome

Courtesy of Cathedral Basilica of Saint Louis Archives

Mosaic pancakes, photo by Verner Burks, FAIA (April 15, 1984). Courtesy of Cathedral Basilica of Saint Louis Archives

Scaffolding for inspection of east transept painting, 1984

Photograph by Richard C. Finke, 1984. Courtesy of Cathedral Basilica of Saint Louis Archives

1984: East Transept Preparation

In 1984, scaffolding was erected to permit the removal of the 1924 al secco mosaic-painting in preparation for the installation of the new mosaics that Arno Heuduck and his staff at Ravenna Mosaics, Inc., in Fredericktown, Missouri, had fabricated, translating the designs of Mary Reardon. "Pancakes" of various colors and shades of glass mosaic were made, selected, and then chiseled to fit the patterns developed from the full-size cartoons of each scene, with all panels carefully created to fit exactly together on the dome surfaces of the cathedral.

Arno Heuduck installing the mosaics of the Resurrection east transept apse, November 6, 1984

Photograph by Richard C. Finke. Courtesy of Cathedral Basilica of Saint Louis Archives

Resurrection east transept apse and arch soffit mosaics, 1984. Designed by Mary Reardon, artist

Photograph by John C. Guenther, FAIA, LEED AP

1984: Resurrection East Transept Mosaic

The mosaics were glued to brown paper-backed segments, in reverse appearance, numbered, packed in boxes, and transported to the cathedral. They were assembled like a gigantic jigsaw puzzle, set in a foundation layer of cement plaster on the structural surfaces and tapped into place, with glass tesserae mosaics set at various angles in an uneven surface so they reflect the light beautifully. With the paper backing removed, grouting filled in the joints. When set, the mosaics were cleaned, revealing one of the most permanent and beautiful wall decorations ever devised.

The mosaic design by Mary Reardon of the east transept dome—The Resurrection—features scenes referring to the multiple appearances of the Risen Christ.

Prominently featured is the appearance in the garden of Christ to Mary Magdalene, who became the Apostle of the resurrection to the Apostles. An angel is seated at an empty tomb. The theme is inscribed at the base of the dome—IF CHRIST HAS NOT RISEN YOUR FAITH IS VAIN.

To the right, Christ has been taken down from the cross, with the disciples taking His dead body to the tomb, while the centurion looks on, declaring—THIS WAS THE SON OF GOD.

To the left, the Risen Christ breaks bread with the disciples of Emmaus, commemorating the death and resurrection of Christ in the Eucharist. The caption reads—THEY KNEW HIM IN THE BREAKING OF THE BREAD.

The east arch soffit mosaic design by Mary Reardon reinforces the resurrection theme of the east transept. To the right, Christ raises Lazarus from the dead—LAZARUS COME FORTH. The scene of Jonah and the whale is also a symbol of resurrection. To the left, Doubting Thomas declares his faith—MY LORD AND MY GOD. The scene of the wheat springing from the seed is a symbol of the new life of the Risen Savior—UNLESS THE SEED DIES. The large cross in the center is a symbol of Christ's death and resurrection.

Arno Heuduck with mosaic panels of the Resurrection east transept apse

Photograph by Verner Burks, FAIA. Courtesy of Cathedral Basilica of Saint Louis Archives

1984: Enhanced Acoustical Performance

The rebuilding of the cathedral organ began on May 31, 1983, with Verner I. Burks, FAIA, designated architect of the cathedral, providing architectural and planning services.

On Thursday evening, July 26, 1984, the Kilgen organ, rebuilt by M. P. Moller, of Hagerstown, Maryland, was rededicated with a concert by cathedral organist Dr. Mario Salvador and the cathedral choir.

Salvador performed the program along with the cathedral's Adult Choir, the Pontifical Children's Choir, and the Archdiocesan Priests' Choir. The program demonstrated the versatility of the rebuilt organ, with organ music ranging from Bach to contemporary works.

Of note, Salvador also played at the dedicatory concert in 1948. He considered this Kilgen organ "one of the great masterpieces of organ building in the United States."

In addition to the rebuilding of the Kilgen organ, the organ setting was dramatically enhanced both visually and musically. With the removal of the organ chamber boxes and bronze grills previously concealing the organ pipes and obstructing the music, the obscured north rose window and mosaics were returned to their original prominence.

The acoustical performance was improved, with "the pipes of the 'great' section and most of the 'pedal' section now unenclosed, allowing them to speak directly into the building, lending greater clarity and depth of tone to the organ," according to the concert program notes.

Monsignor Gannon and Archbishop May received valuable professional guidance from Joseph D. Murphy, FAIA; Verner Burks, FAIA; and G. T. Lawlor, whose firm G. T. Lawlor Construction Co. implemented the design. Dr. Salvador offered valuable candid comments and observations.

The modifications brought the organ up to its full potential.

The restored cathedral organ was ready for the episcopal consecrations of Bishops Edward O'Donnell and Terry Steib on February 10, 1984.

Photograph by Richard C. Finke. Courtesy of Archdiocese of St. Louis Archives

Model of the redesign of the organ with exposed organ pipes by Verner Burks, FAIA

Courtesy of Cathedral Basilica of Saint Louis Museum

Gallery level art glass windows designed by Robert Frei and installed by Emil Frei, Inc. in 1985

Photograph by Nicholas Frei

East transept architrave mosaics (1922–23) level arcade and art glass windows (1985)

Photograph by Serhii Chrucky © Serhii Chrucky I Esto

Gallery level art glass windows designed by Robert Frei and installed by Emil Frei, Inc. in 1985

Photograph by John C. Guenther, FAIA, LEED AP

1985: New Gallery Level Art Glass

In 1985, 24 stained glass windows on the gallery level were designed by Robert Frei and installed by Emil Frei, Inc. The clerestory windows were designed to modulate the light entering the interiors, enhancing the mosaics by decreasing the formerly overpowering glare of the original windows, while uniting the gallery level balcony with the cathedral interior.

The geometric patterns and soft colors of the glass provided interest in design. Of note, the design was composed as three sets of windows, so each group of two is different. The design offered a simple, repeatable process of fabrication, providing variety, efficiency of production, and cost effectiveness, while appearing convincingly rich and Byzantine.

Every piece of glass is identical in design, made using the same silk screen design. The one small pattern was silk-screened over and over to build an entire window. The three-step process required the glass to be fired in the kiln three times. First, strong paint lines were applied on the glass, then half-toned areas were painted by hand, intentionally varied slightly to give the impression of complexity, and finally, the silver stain was applied to yield the yellow-gold coloration.

Monsignor Rowland E. Gannon, rector, called for a meeting with Robert Frei; Joseph D. Murphy, FAIA; Verner Burks, FAIA; Father McNamee, SJ; and Mary Reardon for final review and approval of the design and color.

The new gallery level windows were an important asset and enhanced the interior of the cathedral, especially the mosaics in the nave and transept.

Of note, when one views these clerestory windows, designed by Robert Frei in 1985, in the east and west transepts, the contribution of the Frei family across time is appreciated. Emil Frei, Sr.'s and Ravenna Mosaics' first large commission for the cathedral—August Oetken's 1923 design for the red and gold mosaics of the transept's nave level arcades—now frame the stained glass created and installed by Robert Frei, Frei's grandson.

1984–86: West Transept Preparation

The west half dome and arch soffit al secco mosaic-painting (1925) by Gotthard Bauer representing the Ascension of Christ into heaven, along with his west arch soffit, were removed in anticipation of the Pentecost mosaic design by Mary Agnes Reardon (1912–2002), completed in 1986. This theme was chosen because of the emphasis in contemporary theology on the place of the Holy Spirit in the life of the church and the people of God.

Ravenna Mosaic Company of Fredericktown, Missouri, translated the design and paintings of Mary Reardon into full-size cartoons, detailed mosaic layouts, and panels; prepared the surfaces; and installed the new mosaics in the cathedral. Of note, the mosaics were attached to a brown paper backing in reverse mirror image so that when they were installed in the wet cement mortar and the paper backing was removed, they would appear as intended.

Mosaic craftsman translating full-size cartoon, selecting color mosaics for paper-backed panel in studio, July 29, 1985

Courtesy of Archdiocese of St. Louis Archives

Maquette of Pentecost west half dome mosaic, approved January 14, 1985. Designed by Mary Reardon, artist

Courtesy of Cathedral Basilica of Saint Louis Archives

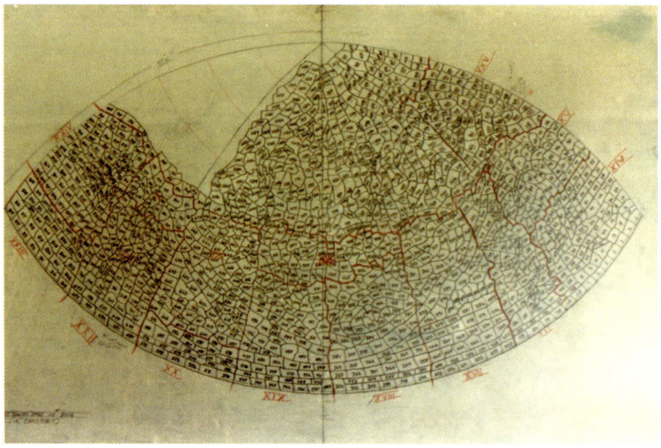

Master key diagram for numbered sections of the Pentecost half dome, August 18, 1986

Courtesy of Archdiocese of St. Louis Archives

Pentecost west transept apse mosaic (1986) Designed by Mary Reardon

Photograph by John C. Guenther, FAIA, LEED AP

Mary Reardon, artist, and Arno Heuduck review full-size cartoon and mosaic panels, July 29, 1985

Photograph by Verner Burks, FAIA. Courtesy of Archdiocese of St. Louis Archives

Meeting at Ravenna Mosaics, Fredericktown, Missouri, October 28, 1985: Msgr. Rowland E. Gannon; Mary A. Reardon; Rev. Maurice McNamee, SJ; Mr. and Mrs. Arno Heuduck; Verner I. Burks, FAIA

Courtesy of Archdiocese of St. Louis Archives

1984–86: Pentecost West Transept Mosaic

The Pentecost mosaic occupies a unique place in the history of Christian art. Reverend Maurice B. McNamee, SJ noted there is no other work of art on this scale devoted to the Descent of the Holy Spirit on Pentecost in the whole history of Christian art. The west half dome and west arch soffit added nearly 4,000 square feet of mosaics.

The Pentecost mosaic depicts the Blessed Mother and the Apostles enveloped in an enormous flame, symbolic of the Holy Spirit. To the right is St. Peter preaching to the Jews, with the walls of Jerusalem in the background, and the inscription—YOU WILL RECEIVE THE GIFT OF THE HOLY SPIRIT. To the left, St. Paul and St. Barnabas preach to the Gentiles, with a sailing ship and a Roman temple representative of Paul's apostolate—I HAVE MADE YOU A LIGHT TO THE NATIONS. The inscription under the half dome reads, I WILL POUR OUT MY SPIRIT ON ALL FLESH. The shape of the flame complements the contour of the half dome. The red, orange, and gold of the flame blend with the red and gold of the main dome of the cathedral.

The west arch soffit depicts Christ's baptism and Ascension into Heaven. To the right, Christ rises into Heaven amid His Apostles. To the left, John the Baptist baptizes Christ, which shows the Trinity—God the Father, the Son, and the Holy Spirit. In the center, a flame on water symbolizes the Holy Spirit and the water of life.

The two half domes express the Pentecost and the Ascension, the two major theological themes in modern Catholic teaching since Vatican II.

The red hat of Archbishop Glennon was raised in the All Souls Chapel by Msgr. Nicholas Brinkman and Fr. Joseph Amsler on March 1945.

Courtesy of Arteaga Photos LTD.

Cathedral Basilica Chapel of Interment

Blessed by Archbishop John L. May, September 28, 1986

Photograph by Richard Finke. Courtesy of Archdiocese of St. Louis Archives

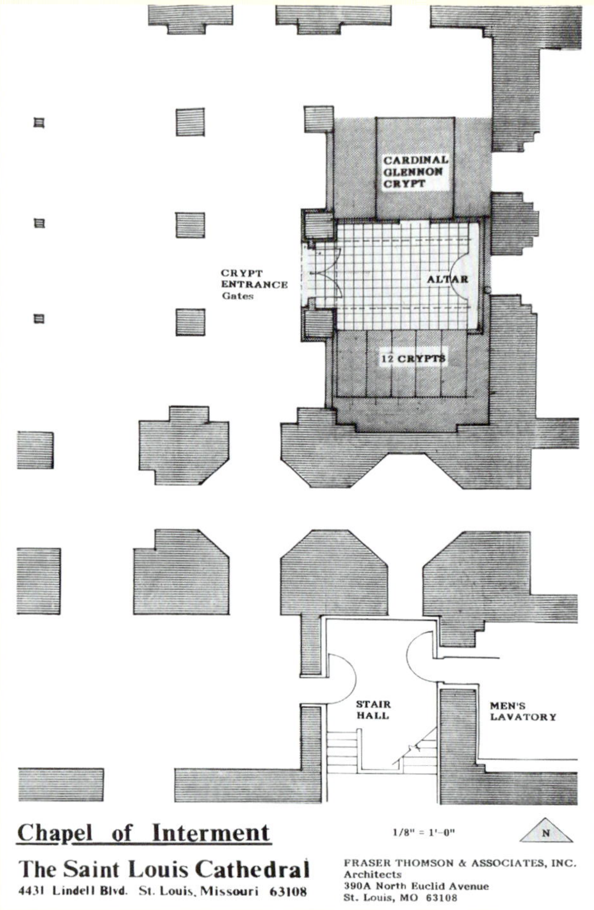

Plan of Chapel of Interment

Fraser Thomson & Associates, Inc., architects and urban planners, 390A North Euclid Avenue, St. Louis, Missouri

Courtesy of Archdiocese of St. Louis Archives

1986: Chapel of Interment

In 1984, Ian Fraser, AIA, and Tom Thomson, AIA, Fraser Thomson & Associates, Inc., architects and urban planners, were commissioned to study five possible options for improvements to the Cathedral of Saint Louis, including the design of the Chapel of Interment to hold the crypt of Cardinal John J. Glennon (1862–1946), with crypts for 12 others. Glennon became archbishop of St. Louis in late 1903, providing significant leadership to the Diocese of St. Louis, and planned and built the great Cathedral of Saint Louis.

The design of the Chapel of Interment features marble walls, a stone floor, and a barrel vault ceiling with indirect cove lighting, with the Chi-Rho with Alpha and Omega mosaic medallion from the 1968 altar serving as a focal point above the altar. This chapel is directly below the All Souls Chapel.

Msgr. Gannon noted this was a much-needed and significant addition to the Cathedral of Saint Louis. He engaged the architects for this project. G. T. Lawlor Construction Co. were the contractors.

1986: Dedication of Restored Altar

Archbishop John L. May blessed the Chapel of Interment at 11:45 a.m. on September 28, 1986, preceding the noontime Mass. Following the Blessing of the Chapel of Interment, Archbishop May proceeded to the front steps of the cathedral to bless three new bronze bells. These had been cast in Holland in July and weighed 1,990 pounds, 1,000 pounds, and 583 pounds respectively. They were lifted into place on Monday September 29, 1986, for their first pealing on October 11, 1986—the 60th anniversary of the cathedral's consecration.

At the Sunday noon Mass, following the homily, Archbishop May dedicated the main altar—the same as the original altar first dedicated by Cardinal Glennon on June 29, 1926, now reconfigured to meet Vatican II guidelines by allowing the celebrant to face the people. The altar and baldacchino were thus restored as the focal point of the cathedral. A temporary marble altar had been in use since 1968 in front of the baldacchino.

The dedication ritual included prayers, the anointing of the top of the altar with the oil of Holy Chrism, and the reinsertion of the same relics of three martyrs of the early Church who were in the original altar—Saints Clement, Aurelius, and Liberatus—and of Pope St. Pius X.

The cathedra, or bishop's chair, was made from the materials taken from the main altar when it was remodeled. It was used for the first time during Easter week, April 14, 1987, by Archbishop May.

The *Grandeur in Granite* video was released on February 28, 1986.

New bells for the cathedral are blessed by Archbishop John L. May, September 28, 1986

Photograph by Richard Finke. Courtesy of Archdiocese of St. Louis Archives

New bells are set atop the cathedral, September 29, 1986

Photograph by Richard Finke. Courtesy of Archdiocese of St. Louis Archives

The restored altar is dedicated by Archbishop John L. May, September 28, 1986.

Photograph by Richard Finke. Courtesy of Archdiocese of St. Louis Archives

1987–88: Historical Bay East Wall Panel

The east and west side wall panels in the Historical Bay were the final mosaics commissioned for the Cathedral of Saint Louis. Mary Reardon designed these panels to harmonize with the mosaics designed by Hildreth Meière (1892–1961) in the Historical Bay at the time of her passing.

The east mosaic panel (1987) memorializes events in the life of Cardinal Ritter and the Church. Ritter's decision to integrate the Catholic schools in St. Louis in 1947, seven years before the Supreme Court's 1954 decision to outlaw segregation in public schools, is commemorated by the sister leading an integrated group of children to his left.

Cardinal Ritter also worked on the document of the Declaration of Religious Liberty in the Second Vatican Council (1962–65) which emphasized the importance of recognizing the sincerity and validity of faith denominations outside the Catholic Church. The Declaration is symbolized by the scroll Ritter is holding, while clergymen of various faiths stand to his right, in front of St. Peter's in Rome.

Mary Reardon's initial design for the east wall panel of local history, 1986. Photograph by Verner Burks, FAIA, August 18, 1986

Courtesy of Archdiocese of St. Louis Archives

Maquette of east wall panel of local history, 1987. Designed by Mary Reardon. Photograph by Verner Burks, FAIA, May 5, 1987

Courtesy of Cathedral Basilica of Saint Louis Archives

East mosaic wall panel of local history, 1987

Courtesy of Cathedral Basilica of Saint Louis Archives

East mosaic panel, designed by Mary Reardon

Photograph by Serhii Chrucky © Serhii Chrucky I Esto

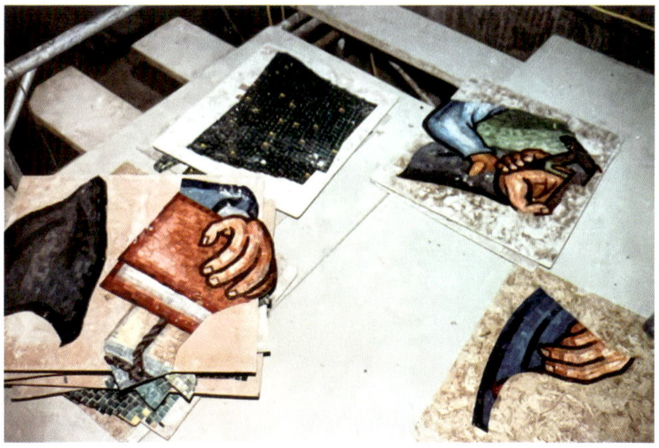

Numbered mosaic sections for west panel on scaffolding, 1988

Photograph by Verner Burks, FAIA. Courtesy of Cathedral Basilica of Saint Louis Archives

Mosaic panel of sister and integrated students in east wall of local history, 1987

Photograph by Verner Burks, FAIA, July 29, 1987. Courtesy of Archdiocese of Saint Louis Archives

1987–88: Historical Bay West Wall Panel

Given the exploration and settlement of the West originating in St. Louis, the city became known as the Gateway to the West, founded on the west bank of the Mississippi River, near the confluence of the Missouri and Illinois Rivers.

The central figure of the west mosaic panel of history is Father Pierre-Jean De Smet, SJ, wearing his buckskin-embroidered jacket, evangelizing to the Indigenous Americans as he traveled the Missouri River. To the left, Father Jaques Marquette, SJ travels with Louis Jolliet down the Mississippi River in 1673, the "Father of the Waters," to evangelize the Illinois Indigenous peoples. To the right, a diocesan priest and a sister from the St. Louis Archdiocese serve as missionaries to the Bolivian people, commemorating the fact that in 1956, the St. Louis Archdiocese was the first in the United States to send missionaries to foreign lands.

With the completion of the east and west mosaic wall panels of local history in 1988, the mosaics, which began in 1915, were now completed after 73 years and generations of dedicated efforts by some of the world's finest artists and craftsmen.

Arno Paul Heuduck (1917–88) died on November 12, 1988, having completed the mosaics in March 1988. Over their lifetimes, he and his father, Paul Johannes Heuduck (1882–1972), artfully crafted and installed in the Cathedral of Saint Louis the largest collection of mosaics in the western hemisphere.

Design paintings of west wall of local history of the Jolliet-Marquette Expedition. Photograph by Verner Burks, FAIA, July 7, 1987. Courtesy of Archdiocese of St. Louis Archives

West mosaic panel. Designed by Mary Reardon

Photograph by Serhii Chrucky © Serhii Chrucky I Esto

Maquette of west wall panel of local history, 1987. Designed by Mary Reardon. Photograph by Verner Burks, FAIA, August 3, 1987. Courtesy of Cathedral Basilica of Saint Louis Archives

Mosaic panels, west wall of local history, Marquette and Jolliet Expedition. Photograph by Verner Burks, FAIA, December 12, 1987

Courtesy of Archdiocese of St. Louis Archives

Mosaic west wall panel of local history of foreign missions, 1988. Photograph by Verner Burks, FAIA, February 19, 1988

Courtesy of Archdiocese of St. Louis Archives

Arno Heuduck's table and tools

Courtesy of Cathedral Basilica of Saint Louis Museum

Photograph by John C. Guenther, FAIA, LEED AP

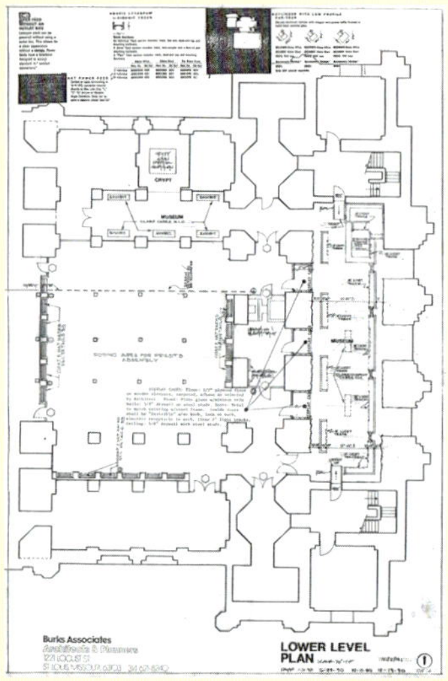

Floor plan of Mosaic Museum by Burks Associates, Architects & Planners, February 7, 1991

Courtesy of Archdiocese of St. Louis Archives

1990–92: Mosaic Museum

With the mosaics completed in 1988, the Cathedral of Saint Louis experienced a growth in visitors. It was decided that a museum telling the story of making the mosaics would greatly add to the visitor experience and appreciation of what they were seeing. In 1990, Archbishop John L. May announced the new Mosaic Museum, which would be housed in the cathedral undercroft.

The museum planning was carried out by the Archdiocesan Commission for Sacred Art. Verner Burks, FAIA, architect, planned the museum. He received guidance from Father Maurice McNamee, SJ, commission member and curator of Saint Louis University's Cupples House, who planned the contents. G. T. Lawlor Construction Co. was selected to renovate the museum in 1991.

The museum ceiling was left exposed so that visitors can see the structural components. Massive gray stone walls were left bare so the huge foundations remained visible. The new museum houses an extensive photographic display on the history and artistic style of both the cathedral and its predecessor, the Basilica of St. Louis, King of France (Old Cathedral). Also on exhibit are liturgical vestments and vessels of historical and artistic significance.

The most distinctive feature is a series of displays, photographic and three-dimensional, showing the complete process of making mosaics, from the design by the artist to the fabrication and installation by the mosaicist. A display of Arno Heuduck's worktable, tools, and materials shows how the mosaicist assembled an average of 500 bits of glass tesserae mosaics in each square foot of finished mosaic. More than 90 percent of the mosaics were installed by the late Heuduck and his father, Paul Heuduck, who came to St. Louis from Berlin in 1923, and Ravenna Mosaics, Inc., founded by Emil Frei, Sr. with Pühl & Wagner of Berlin (later the Ravenna Company).

The new museum opened on Sunday, October 25, 1992, with a reception from 1 p.m. to 5 p.m. In 1992, 150,000 visitors walked through the cathedral to view the Western world's largest collection of mosaics—an estimated 41.5 million bits of colored glass mosaics, covering 83,000 square feet, with some 7,000 colors used, including 200 different shades of gold.

1990–92: Arno Heuduck Honored

In February 1990, workers put a shine on a section of the Cathedral of Saint Louis. Mosaics at the cathedral require periodic cleaning, according to Father James R. Michler, associate pastor. Scaffolding was set up to reach many out-of-the-way areas and the workers spent part of a week there.

A lighting study was undertaken by William Tao & Associates on January 16, 1991, to address the necessary changes to increase lighting intensity over the areas occupied by the assembly, cosmetic changes to improve the appearance of the cathedral, and precautionary changes to replace outdated equipment and provide more economical equipment to save on yearly expenses.

In 1992, Dr. John Romeri became the third organist-choirmaster (1992–2010). He directed the Cathedral Choir, Schola, and founded the Archdiocesan Adult and Children's Choirs. He also began St. Louis Cathedral Concerts in 1992, which brought many of the world's greatest performers to St. Louis and the cathedral, reaching a larger community. Under his direction, the choirs made several singing tours to Italy, England, Germany, and Austria.

On September 15, 1992, the American Institute of Architects St. Louis Chapter awarded its Craftsmanship Lifetime Achievement Award to mosaicist Arno Heuduck, who had completed the vast mosaic interiors of the Cathedral of Saint Louis just eight months before his death in November 1988 at the age of 77, after undergoing chemotherapy for liver cancer. During the last 18 months of his life, he completed the east and west half domes and two arch soffits of the cathedral's transept. Following the completion of those works, the east and west mosaic panels of local history were finished in 1988. The award was accepted by Arno's widow, Delpha Heuduck.

Arno and his father, Paul Heuduck, placed most of the 41.5 million pieces of gold and colored glass tesserae mosaics in the cathedral, resulting in the largest collection of mosaics in the Western world. Arno skillfully interpreted the drawings of the various commissioned artists, executing them in more than 7,000 shades of colored glass and 24-carat gold mosaics. He carefully placed the mosaics, which averaged 500 pieces per square foot, into wet cement mortar at angles to catch the light.

Arno Heuduck. Courtesy of Archdiocese of St. Louis Archives

St. Louis Cathedral Concerts. Courtesy of Archdiocese of St. Louis Archives

Dr. John A. Romeri
Cathedral of Saint Louis
Organist-Choirmaster (1992–2010)
Courtesy of the Office for Divine Worship, Archdiocese of St. Louis

1994–97: Cathedral Basilica of Saint Louis

Justin Francis Rigali (1935–)

Courtesy of Archdiocese of St. Louis Archives

The Ombrellino or umbrella is a special symbol of Basilica Designation for the Cathedral of Saint Louis.

Courtesy of the Archdiocese of St. Louis Archives

On January 25, 1994, Pope John Paul II named Justin Francis Rigali as the new archbishop of the Archdiocese of St. Louis. Rigali was installed as the eighth bishop and seventh archbishop of St. Louis on March 16, 1994, serving here until 2003, when he was appointed the eighth archbishop of Philadelphia by Pope John Paul II on July 15, 2003. He was installed as archbishop on October 7, 2003, and elevated to the College of Cardinals on October 21, 2003.

Rigali was the successor to Archbishop John L. May, who resigned as archbishop for health reasons on December 9, 1992, after celebrating the silver jubilee of his ordination as bishop with 10,000 of his loving flock in attendance at the St. Louis Arena on November 22, 1992. On March 24, 1994, a week after his successor's installation, May died peacefully at a St. Louis nursing home. Archbishop May (1922–94) is interred in the Cathedral Basilica Chapel of Interment.

Within his first 500 days, Archbishop Rigali prepared the groundwork for the strategic pastoral plan for the archdiocese.

In 1995, Archbishop Rigali announced that the archdiocese would assume full responsibility for the administration of Kenrick-Glennon Seminary, after 177 years of collaboration with the Vincentian community running the seminary.

On January 5, 1997, the Edward and Eileen Roehr Memorial Console and Organ Restoration Project was dedicated at the cathedral's 10 a.m. Mass, with an organ recital by Charles Callahan, composer and restoration project consultant. The cost of the main organ work was $280,000.

On April 4, 1997, Pope John Paul II honored the Cathedral of Saint Louis by making it a basilica, a place of worship of special distinction.

On October 19, 1997, a Solemn Eucharistic Celebration was held for the 150th anniversary of the elevation of the Diocese of St. Louis to the Metropolitan Archdiocese of St. Louis and the designation of the Cathedral of Saint Louis to the rank of basilica, with His Eminence Jan Pieter Cardinal Schotte, CJCM, special envoy of His Holiness Pope John Paul II, presiding. The colloquially known New Cathedral and Mother Church of the archdiocese became the Cathedral Basilica of Saint Louis.

The Ombrellino—an eight-sided umbrella—and the Tintinnabulum—a processional shrine—were designed and fabricated by Stadelmaier Nijmegen B.V. of Holland and Europe.

1998: Ombrellino Crest

Given the basilica designation by Pope John Paul II on April 4, 1997, and his anticipated visit in 1999, Emil Frei, Inc. was commissioned in 1998 to create a basilica crest. The crest took the form of an ombrellino (Italian for umbrella), signifying that the cathedral is a basilica.

The crest was designed by Robert Frei in conjunction with Stephen Frei. The top is in the shape and colors of the ombrellino found inside the Cathedral Basilica of Saint Louis. At the base, an inscription reads, PER JESUM CHRISTUM—Through Jesus Christ. Between, a shield features the Chi Rho flanked by two fleur-de-lis above a wavy line, representative of Christ, St. Louis, and the Mississippi River, on a red background. A gold crown is representative of Louis IX (1214–70), also known as Saint Louis, King of France, alongside a cross in gold with an M representing Mary at the foot of the cross, both in a field of blue. Two keys, representative of the keys to the Kingdom of Heaven given to Peter, form an X behind the shield. It is composed of glazed ceramic tile set in a metal frame.

The crest was completed and installed just before the papal visit on January 26-27, 1999.

Robert Frei designed and crafted the basilica crest in conjunction with Stephen Frei in 1998.

Courtesy of Emil Frei & Associates

The Archdiocesan Choir and the Cathedral Choir made their first European singing tour to Italy in 1998. They performed in Venice, Florence, Assisi, and Rome. In St. Peter's Basilica, they sang for Pope John Paul II on the Feast of Saints Peter and Paul.

Courtesy of Cathedral Basilica of Saint Louis Museum

The basilica crest installed above the south entry doors in 1999

Photograph by John C. Guenther, FAIA, LEED AP

"Seal of the Millennium"

Courtesy of Emil Frei & Associates

Robert Frei holding up the seal to be blessed before installation on the central door in the vestibule, which happened at the end of the papal mass on Visit by Pope John Paul II's exit

Photograph © Vatican Media

South portal entrance

South portico entrance to the Cathedral Basilica of Saint Louis with the basilica crest installed above the south entry doors in 1999, which were sealed for one year by the "Seal of the Millennium" and interior seal until Christmas 1999

Photograph by John C. Guenther, FAIA, LEED AP

January 26-27, 1999: Seal of the Millennium

The "Seal of the Millennium" was made from ceramics and glazed. It was then kiln-fired to make permanent the colors. It was mounted on the exterior of the central portico's door, facing the street. It sealed the door for one year and was to be broken at Christmas in 1999—the new millennium.

The first version of the "Seal of the Millennium" did not include the gold background. A second all-gold layer was added behind the circular seal to enhance the contrast with the exterior wood doors.

A second seal, facing inward, was prepared for the interior of the central door, with Pope John Paul II's name on it. Both seals were made solely by Robert Frei.

Neither seal was broken, even though duplicates were supplied for the museum.

On January 27, 1999, Pope John Paul II prayed in the Chapel of Our Lady.

Photograph © Vatican Media

1999 Papal Visit by Pope John Paul II, January 26–27, 1999

Evening prayer at the Cathedral Basilica of Saint Louis on January 27, 1999

Photograph by Jeanne Rohner. Courtesy of Archdiocese of St. Louis Archives

1999 Papal Visit by Pope John Paul II, January 26-27, 1999

Evening prayer at the Cathedral Basilica of Saint Louis on January 27, 1999

Photograph by Mark Kempf. Courtesy of Archdiocese of St. Louis Archives

January 26-27, 1999: Papal Visit

Nineteen ninety-nine was an immensely significant year for the Archdiocese of St. Louis, as it would host a visit from a pope who would be named a saint. His Holiness Pope John Paul II made a pastoral visit to St. Louis on January 26 and 27, 1999—an event unmatched in the memory of St. Louisans.

For these days, St. Louis was the heart of the Church. In the person of Pope John Paul II, Peter, the Vicar of Christ, was in our midst. The 32-hour visit to the archdiocese was arguably the single most significant historical event in the life of the local Church since its founding in 1826. Events included a solemn Mass of the Sacred Heart at the downtown sports dome on Wednesday, January 27, and solemn high Vespers that evening at the Cathedral Basilica of Saint Louis.

Pope John Paul II completed his passage to America at the invitation of his longtime collaborator, Archbishop Rigali, with a Pastoral Visit to St. Louis following his visit to Mexico City and the shrine of the patroness of America, Our Lady of Guadalupe, to give the world the document "The Church in America" on January 22, 1999.

1999 Papal Visit by Pope John Paul II, January 26–27, 1999

Evening prayer at the Cathedral Basilica of Saint Louis on January 27, 1999

Photograph by Jeanne Rohner. Courtesy of Archdiocese of St. Louis Archives

Sculpture titled *The Angel of Harmony* (1999)

Photograph by John C. Guenther, FAIA, LEED AP

1999: *The Angel of Harmony*

The Angel of Harmony sculpture was installed in 1999. This remarkable sculpture was created by the Polish sculptor Wiktor Szostalo and is dedicated to harmony, peace, and racial justice.

"The African American features will depart from traditional images of angels with European features in order to emphasize the universality of God's love for all people," said Senior Auxiliary Bishop Edward K. Braxton, an African American bishop who suggested the renowned artist Szostalo to Archbishop Justin Rigali and oversaw preparation of the work.

Archbishop Rigali noted, "Our hope is that this sculpture will be a symbol of the Catholic Church's commitment to the city and the great diversity of people who live here. It is an extension of our efforts to . . . create harmony, peace, and justice among people of diverse racial and cultural backgrounds."

Artist Szostalo, a native of Poland, who has always looked for "art with a cause," made the sculpture in his Chouteau Avenue studio, forming more than 2,000 pounds of stainless steel and high-resistance resins and pigments in *The Angel of Harmony*.

The dramatic sculpture depicts a towering angel with distinctive African American features, with powerful wings and outstretched arms. The angel's arms have wind chimes and they are spread to protect three children of diverse ethnic and racial backgrounds playing a "Hymn of Peace" on various instruments. The European American youth is playing an African drum, the Hispanic boy is playing a Peruvian pan flute, and the Asian American girl is playing an Oriental wind chime.

The base of the sculpture is inscribed with quotations from the New Testament, Pope John Paul II, and Dr. Martin Luther King, Jr.

This sculpture is thought to be the first time a Catholic diocese has commissioned a work in which the messenger of God appears as an African American.

Wiktor Szostalo, a native of Poland and artist and sculptor in St. Louis, and Senior Auxiliary Bishop Edward K. Braxton, African American bishop who oversaw preparation of the work

Courtesy of Archdiocese of St. Louis Archives

The sculpture was a gift to the Archdiocese of St. Louis from Adelaide Schlafly in memory of her late husband, Daniel Lyons Schlafly, who died in 1997 after dedicating much of his life and resources to the cause of racial justice and peace.

Dr. Mario Salvador, who arrived in 1940 to become the second director of music, organist, and choir director for the Cathedral of Saint Louis, a position he held from 1940 to 1992, died in 1999.

His recitals filled the cathedral, especially for the organ dedication in 1949 and rededication in 1984. His choirs included the men and boys and a priest choir.

2004–08: Shrine to the Sacred Heart

Raymond Leo Burke was named archbishop of St. Louis on December 2, 2003, and installed as the ninth bishop and eighth archbishop of St. Louis on January 26, 2004, succeeding then-Cardinal Justin Francis Rigali. Archbishop Burke was presented with the pallium on June 29, 2004, by Pope John Paul II.

In 2006, a life-size replica in bronze of Michelangelo's *Pietá*, cast in 1982 by the Marinelli Bronze Foundry, Florence, Italy, was loaned from the owners, Legacy Sculptures and Renaissance Sculptures, LLC, to the Cathedral Basilica of Saint Louis. It is one of two pieces being exhibited in North America.

On Sunday, January 7, 2007, on the 10th anniversary of the dedication of the Roehr Memorial Console, the dome organ was dedicated to the memory of Margaret Mary and Charles Callahan, Sr. The concert was played by organist Dr. Charles Callahan, Jr. The Archdiocesan Choir of St. Louis also participated in this dedication. The organ now had 118 ranks and 7,621 pipes.

The Shrine to the Sacred Heart, located in the west transept of the Cathedral Basilica of Saint Louis, features a mosaic image of the Sacred Heart handcrafted by the Fabbrica di San Pietro, the Vatican mosaic studio. The shrine was conceived by Archbishop Burke to foster the devotion of the faithful to the Sacred Heart. On June 17, 2007, he consecrated the Shrine to the Sacred Heart, designed by Duncan G. Stroik of the School of Architecture at the University of Notre Dame. It is the most recent addition to the Cathedral Basilica of Saint Louis.

On Saturday, September 15, 2007, a life-size bronze bust of St. Francis de Sales in the Jubilee Prayer Garden was dedicated by Archbishop Burke. The sculpture was installed in memory of Delphine Madill (1905–2003), a lifelong member of the Cathedral Basilica parish and foundress of the Society of St. Francis de Sales in the United States in 1947, marking the 60th anniversary of the Society's founding. Father Anthony Brakin of Chicago, a theologian and sculptor, was commissioned to make the bust. Bob Cradock, of Architectural Stone Inc. in St. Louis, donated the black granite pedestal and installed the piece.

In January 2008, Archbishop Burke, tireless in his efforts to foster vocations to the priesthood and religious life, and credited with helping to make the seminary program at Kenrick-Glennon one of the finest in the country, academically, spiritually, and pastorally, announced the start of a major renovation and addition for Kenrick-Glennon Seminary.

Burke's farewell Mass in the Archdiocese of St. Louis was held in the Cathedral Basilica of Saint Louis on August 17, 2008.

Raymond Leo Burke (1948–). Mark Kempf Photography

Courtesy of Archdiocese of St. Louis Archives

Shrine to the Sacred Heart (2007)

Photograph by Serhii Chrucky © Serhii Chrucky I Esto

St. Francis de Sales sculpture (2007)

Photograph by John C. Guenther, FAIA, LEED AP

Restoration of St. Joseph Chapel at Kenrick-Glennon Seminary (2014–15). McCreary Architects. BSI Constructors

Photograph by John C. Guenther, FAIA, LEED AP

Archbishop Robert James Carlson (1944–)

Courtesy of Archdiocese of St. Louis Archives

Auxiliary Bishop Robert Joseph Hermann (1934–). Bishop Hermann presents awards to Girls Scouts on Presentation Sunday, March 9, 2009. Photograph by Richard Finke. Courtesy of Archdiocese of St. Louis Archives

2008–20: Kenrick-Glennon Seminary

In 2009, after Burke had been called to Rome, Bishop Robert Joseph Hermann, auxiliary bishop of Saint Louis since he was appointed by Pope John Paul II on October 16, 2002, was appointed as interim administrator of the diocese until April 21, 2009, when Bishop Robert Carlson was named archbishop. Bishop Hermann led the archdiocese as apostolic administrator in concert with the archbishop-elect until Archbishop Robert J. Carlson was installed as archbishop of St. Louis at the Cathedral Basilica of Saint Louis on June 10, 2009. He received the pallium from Pope Benedict XVI on June 29, 2009, in a ceremony at St. Peter's Basilica.

In 2009, the Future Capital Campaign was conducted in the Archdiocese of St. Louis for the purpose of financing the renovation and addition for the Kenrick-Glennon Seminary building.

The renovations and building addition required the seminary to relocate for a year and a half, from the start of the 2011–12 school year through Christmas 2012. Work included a building addition; site improvements; roofing repair; window replacement; masonry restoration; mechanical, plumbing, and fire protection infrastructure updates; and extensive interior renovations, including much-needed improvements to classrooms, the library, faculty and administrative offices, meeting and lounge spaces, dining facilities, and student residences.

The Kenrick-Glennon seminarians moved back to Shrewsbury for the second semester of the 2012–13 school year. The project designed by CannonDesign of St. Louis won an award from the American Institute of Architects St. Louis Chapter.

In 2010, Carlson began "Alive in Christ" to strengthen and grow Catholic education in the Archdiocese of St. Louis and grow Catholic schools to be alive in Christ.

Archbishop Carlson turned 75 on June 30, 2019. As required by canon law, he submitted his letter of resignation/retirement to the Pope. He continued to shepherd the faithful of the "Rome of the West" until the installation of his successor on August 25, 2020.

2008–20: Organ Restoration Completed

In 2011, Dr. Horst Buchholz became the fourth director of sacred music at the cathedral and the Archdiocese of St. Louis. He received his first musical training in a boys' choir in his native Germany and studied organ and sacred music at the Berlin College of Church Music and the University of Arts, and he received his doctor of music degree in conducting from the Indiana University School of Music. His predecessors included Mr. William Diebels (1915–39), Dr. Mario Salvador, AAGO (1940–92), and Dr. John Romeri, AAGO, ChM (1992–2010)—the first three directors of music and organists for the Cathedral Basilica of Saint Louis.

In 2011, the final phase of the restoration of the organ was completed, when the small two-keyboard console in the gallery was replaced with a five-manual console acquired from St. Bartholomew Episcopal Church in New York City. It is one of only two of the five manual consoles built by the Aeolian-Skinner Company. Having a full console in the gallery returns the organ to its original state. It was refurbished by the Emery Brothers of Pennsylvania. The five new keyboards were constructed by the Colby Company of Kentucky to match the original Aeolian-Skinner keyboards.

The cathedral had two duplicate consoles from 1915 to 1949. In 1949 the main organ was moved downstairs and was only controlled from the main console. The restoration and installation of the console was made possible by a donation from cathedral parishioner Brian Abel Ragen.

In 2012, Cignal Systems installed a new sound system for the cathedral with speakers installed on the underside of the pews to improve the acoustical legibility for parishioners.

In 2014, Archbishop Robert J. Carlson consecrated the Archdiocese of St. Louis to the Holy Spirit.

Monsignor Henry Breier was transferred to the Cathedral Basilica of Saint Louis to serve as its rector on June 28, 2019.

Five-manual Aeolian-Skinner organ console in South Gallery

Photograph by Serhii Chrucky © Serhii Chrucky I Esto

Reverend Monsignor Henry J. Breier, appointed rector, Cathedral Basilica of Saint Louis, on June 28, 2019

Courtesy of Cathedral Basilica of Saint Louis

Dr. Horst Buchholz

Fourth music director, archdiocese/cathedral, serving between 2011 and 2021

Courtesy of Dr. Horst Buchholz

Organ console and choir in South Gallery beneath south rose window Designed by the Tiffany Company

Photograph by Serhii Chrucky © Serhii Chrucky | Esto

View from the choir loft of the Cathedral Basilica of Saint Louis

Photograph by Sam Fentress, © SAM FENTRESS PHOTOGRAPHY

Thirty-seven 180-watt narrow distribution LED flood and accent lights attached to a suspended armature project light through the oculus of the central dome. Photograph by Randy Burkett, FIALD, LC. Courtesy of Reed Burkett Lighting Design (RBLD)

Andrew Kreigh, director of sacred music for the Archdiocese of St. Louis and Cathedral Basilica of Saint Louis. Courtesy of the Archdiocese of St. Louis/*St. Louis Review*

Archbishop Mitchell T. Rozanski (1958–)

Courtesy of Archdiocese of St. Louis

2020–25: Transformational Lighting

On June 10, 2020, Pope Francis named Mitchell T. Rozanski as the 10th archbishop for the Archdiocese of St. Louis. His installation Mass was on August 25, 2020. Prior to this, Bishop Rozanski served as bishop for the Diocese of Springfield, Massachusetts (2014–20), having been appointed by Pope Francis.

Andrew Kreigh was named in June 2022 as director of sacred music for the Archdiocese of St. Louis and Cathedral Basilica of Saint Louis. He is the fifth director of music in the Cathedral Basilica's 109-year history.

In September 2023, Reed Burkett Lighting Design (RBLD) completed the transformational lighting design project to illuminate the interior of the Cathedral Basilica of Saint Louis.

The new lighting design by RBLD enhanced the day-to-day experience in the space and achieved a striking revelation of the mosaics, artwork, sculptures, and architecture not previously viewed in such color and detail. In some areas of the nave and transepts, the light was elevated by nearly 300 percent, allowing formerly invisible details to be enjoyed for the first time. Of note, while the lighting levels were increased dramatically, the system's energy consumption is 87 percent lower! Maintenance cycles are greatly improved, as the LED fixtures have 50,000 hours of rated life. Schaeffer Electric installed the new lighting system.

All new lighting is controlled through a centralized DMX system, with presets established for daily and special events. Docents leading visitor tours use wireless devices to activate presets that highlight specific art and architecture, enhancing the mosaic storytelling experience.

Monsignor Henry Breier noted, "If you've been to the cathedral but you haven't been back since the new lighting, one of things that you've never seen before are the mosaics in all their glory."

2020–25: National Eucharistic Pilgrimage

On Sunday, July 7, 2024, a Mass was held in the Cathedral Basilica of Saint Louis for the National Eucharistic Pilgrimage for those walking from San Francisco, California, on their way to the 10th National Eucharistic Congress—the first in 83 years—held in Indianapolis, Indiana, from July 17 to July 21, 2024, with 62,500 in attendance. The Perpetual Pilgrims walked across the country, taking four routes—the Marian route (north), starting from the Mississippi River headwaters, Lake Itaska, Minnesota; the Saint Elizabeth Ann Seton route (east), starting from New Haven, Connecticut; the Saint Juan Diego route (south), starting from Brownsville, Texas; and the Saint Junipero Serra route (west), starting from San Francisco, California.

Before the arrival of the Perpetual Pilgrams from San Francisco, the Cathedral Basilica's baldacchino and the walls of the sanctuary received a six-week-long deep cleaning. A uniquely engineered outrigger boom suspended five stories high provided the cleaners' access. A chemical wash was applied to clean away almost 100 years of soot and grime, revealing the original creamy marble.

The cleaning project was done by John Tiedemann Inc., which specializes in cleaning and decorating churches. The project corresponded with the Cathedral Basilica's new interior lighting. Msgr. Breier noted, "Throughout the entire cathedral, you will be able to see things we haven't seen before."

Baldacchino of Cathedral Basilica of Saint Louis

Photograph by Serhii Chrucky © Serhii Chrucky I Esto

National Eucharistic Pilgrimage Mass

Cathedral Basilica of Saint Louis, Sunday July 7, 2024

Photograph by John C. Guenther, FAIA, LEED AP

2020–25: Restorations

In December 2024, the restoration of the Mosaic Museum, located in the lower level of the Cathedral Basilica, was completed. The museum contains several displays depicting the design and installation of the mosaics, the original Kilgen organ console, the throne used during the visit of Pope John Paul II, and a collection of historic vestments and precious objects used in the various rites of the Church.

In September 2024, *The Angel of Harmony* sculpture, designed by Wiktor Szostalo in 1999, was badly damaged by a man tampering with construction equipment. A boom lift had been dropped onto the 11-foot sculpture, knocking it off its pedestal.

Szostalo, now 72, restored the sculpture, which emphasizes a "theme of harmony, peace, and racial justice." Szostalo received the damaged sculpture at his Granite City, Illinois, studio around Christmas of 2024. The head of the boy with the drum was nearly torn off and his torso deformed. The sitting girl's legs were twisted. The angel's wings were bent out of shape, with the wind chimes dented and pointing in all directions. The steel base of the sculpture was twisted.

By late February of 2025, the figures of the boy and girl were repaired and ready to be reattached to the rest of the sculpture. Grinding and polishing of the reassembled figures followed, returning the sculpture as closely as possible to its original form. The work was completed in the spring of 2025.

The Angel of Harmony base features three inscriptions:

"Blessed are the merciful, for they shall obtain mercy. Blessed are the pure of heart; for they shall see God. Blessed are the peacemakers; for they shall be called children of God." —Matthew 5:7–9

"Love is the only force capable of transforming an enemy into a friend." —Dr. Martin Luther King, Jr.

"America will remain a beacon of freedom for the world as long as it stands by those moral truths which are at the very heart of its historical experience. And so, America, if you want peace, work for justice. If you want justice, defend life. If you want life, embrace the truth revealed by God." —Pope John Paul II, St. Louis, January 27, 1999

As sculptor Wiktor Szostalo reflected on the repair of the sculpture, he noted it can be encouragement for all of us, saying, "Even the attempts at creating harmony may be attacked; maybe there will be folks trying to interrupt it, but we just get up and move on."

The Angel of Harmony was reinstalled on May 20, 2025.

Sculptor Wiktor Szostalo worked on his *The Angel of Harmony* stainless steel sculpture on February 27, 2025, outside his studio in Granite City, Illinois, to restore it after it was vandalized in September 2024.

Photograph by Jacob Wiegand. Courtesy of the Archdiocese of St. Louis/*St. Louis Review*

2025: A Future Pope Walked Among Us: The First Pope from the United States

On May 8, 2025, Pope Leo XIV, who was born Robert Francis Prevost on September 14, 1955, in Chicago, Illinois, became the head of the Catholic Church and sovereign of the Vatican City State. He was elected pope in the conclave following the death of Pope Francis on April 21, 2025.

Robert Prevost completed his secondary education at St. Augustine Seminary High School, a minor seminary in Holland, Michigan, in 1973. In 1977, he earned a bachelor of science degree in mathematics from Villanova University, which was founded by the Augustinians.

In September 1977, he joined the Order of Saint Augustine as a novice, residing at Immaculate Conception Church/St. Henry Church (which merged in January 1977) in St. Louis, Missouri, for one year. His first vows were taken in September 1978, with his solemn vows taken in August 1981. He was ordained a priest by Archbishop Jean Jadot for the Augustinians in Rome on June 19, 1982.

He went on to serve as the prior general of the Order of Saint Augustine (2001–13), titular bishop of Sufar (2014–15), apostolic administrator of Chiclayo (2014–15), bishop of Chiclayo (2015–23), cardinal deacon of Santa Monica (2023–25), prefect of the Dicastery for Bishops (2023–25), president of the Pontifical Commission for Latin America (2023–25), and cardinal bishop of Albano (2025).

As his friends reflected on the young man they knew, they remembered him as smart, unassuming, and contemplative.

Pope Leo XIV is an American and a naturalized citizen of Peru as a result of his many years of missionary service there. He is the first pope from the United States or from Peru, and the first pope from the Order of Saint Augustine. He seeks to build bridges to bring peace and unite the world.

With Pope Leo XIV having spent a year here in St. Louis in formation as a novice, the St. Louis moniker as "The Rome of the West" has taken on new significance.

Of note, his predecessor, Pope Leo XII, divided the Louisiana Territory into two dioceses—New Orleans and St. Louis, thus founding the Archdiocese of St. Louis on July 18, 1826.

Barnett, Haynes & Barnett, architects of St. Louis, designed the Gothic Revival–style Immaculate Conception Church (built 1904–8) as they prepared their award-winning design of 1906 for the Cathedral Basilica of Saint Louis.

Immaculate Conception/St. Henry Church, 3120 Lafayette Ave., St. Louis, Missouri

Brother Ambrose of the Dominican Order views the church where Robert Prevost, an Augustinian novice, and now Pope Leo XIV, once served this community, in 1977–78.

Photograph by John C. Guenther, FAIA, LEED AP

Pope Leo XIV greets all those gathered in St. Peter's Square in his first public appearance as Pope, May 8, 2025.

Photograph © Vatican Media

Postcard courtesy of the St. Louis Building Arts Foundation Library (National Building Arts Center)

"St. Ann's Orphan Asylum stood at the northwest corner of Page and Union from 1904 until the late 1970s, when it was demolished. Operated by the Roman Catholic Church, the asylum relocated to the city's west end from a downtown location at 10th and O'Fallon Streets. The building permit dates to June 22, 1904, and lists a construction cost of $200,000 and the architects as Barnett, Haynes & Barnett."

Michael R. Allen

Lost: St. Ann's Orphan Asylum

preservationresearch.com/architecture/lost-st-anns-orphan-asylum/

February 3, 2009

Postscript

As the author of this book, I am constantly fascinated by the interconnectivity of history.

Barnett, Haynes & Barnett were the architects of the Cathedral Basilica of Saint Louis, the main subject of this book, having been selected by Archbishop Glennon and the Building Committee as winners of the new cathedral competition on February 12, 1906.

Two years earlier, with a building permit dating to June 22, 1904, Barnett, Haynes & Barnett were the architects and designers of St. Ann's Orphan Asylum.

I was born there and was adopted from there at 9 weeks of age in 1954, through Catholic Charities. I will be forever grateful to my parents, Carl and Dolores Guenther, for adopting me and bringing me into their loving, faith-filled home, forming, shaping, and loving me. I am truly blessed.

John C. Guenther, FAIA, LEED AP
Author, *The Cathedral Basilica of Saint Louis: An Illustrated Timeline*

Caritas

Mosaic in east arch soffit of Local History, which recognizes the work of Catholic Charities

Photograph by John C. Guenther, FAIA, LEED AP

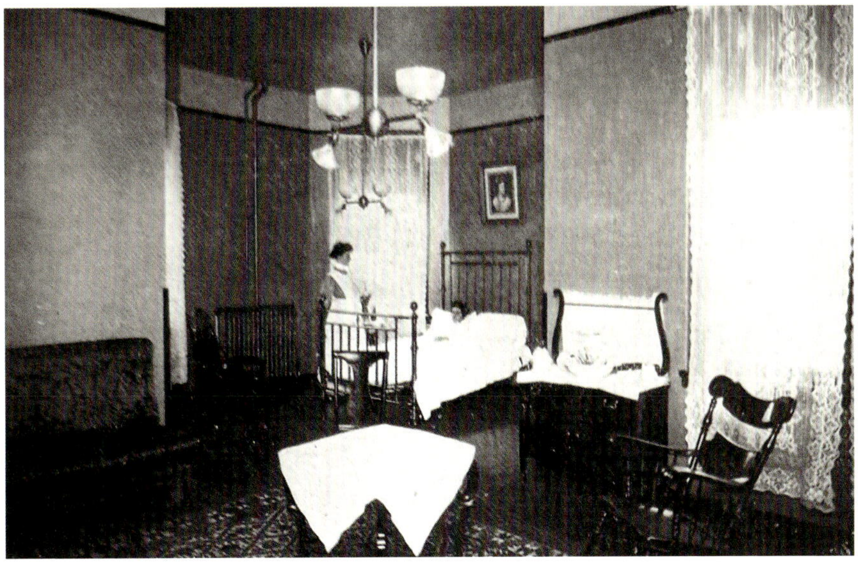

St. Ann's Orphan Asylum and Orphan's Home—a ward room. From *Notable Catholic Institutions* (1911)

Courtesy of St. Louis Public Library–Central Library

Plan of Cathedral Basilica of Saint Louis

1. Vestibule—Mosaics of St. Louis, King of France
2. Central Dome
3. Chair of Archbishop of St. Louis
4. High Altar and Baldacchino
5. Arch of Triumph
6. Arch of Creation
7. Resurrection—East Transept
8. Arch of Sanctification
9. Pentecost—West Transept
10. Arch of the Last Judgment
11. Pendentive of Saint Thomas Aquinas
12. Pendentive of Saint Ambrose
13. Last Supper Mosaic (Gallery Level)
14. Passover Scene (Gallery Level)
15. Pendentive of Saint Cyril of Jerusalem
16. Pendentive of Saint John Chrysostom
17. Pendentive of The Angel of the New Law
18. Pendentive of The Angel of the Old Law
19. Pulpit
20. Stairs to Mosaic Museum and Chapel of Interment
21. Blessed Sacrament Chapel
22. Corridor of Coats of Arms
23. Sacristy
24. Kilgen Organ
25. Our Lady's Chapel
26. All Saints Chapel
27. All Souls Chapel
28. Dome of Local History
29. Shrine to the Sacred Heart
30. Baptismal Font

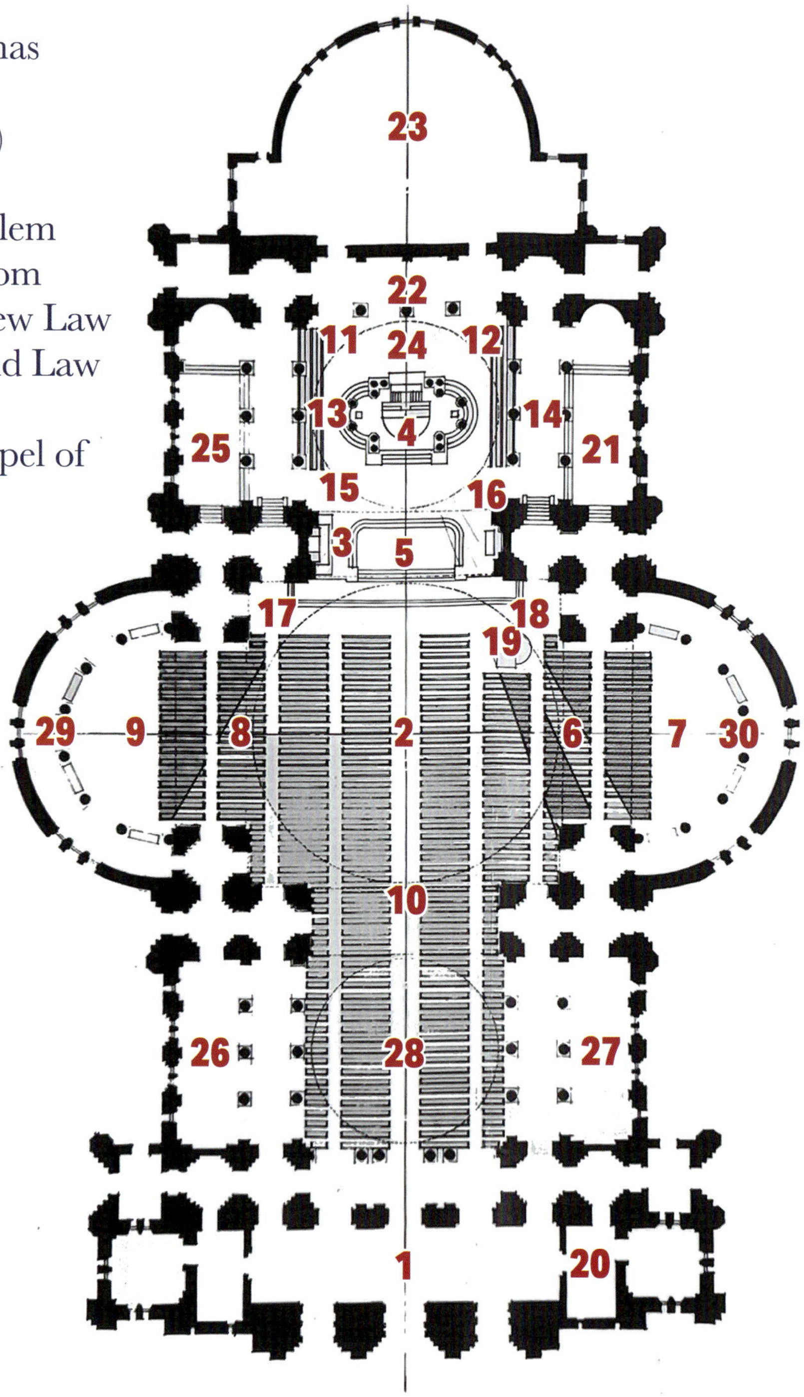

The George Kilgen and Son church and parlor pipe organs company

Established in New York in 1851 and in St. Louis in 1873. Courtesy of Archdiocese of St. Louis Archives

Bibliography

Archdiocese of St. Louis: Three Centuries of Catholicism 1700-2000. Archdiocese of St. Louis, 2001.

The Art Spirit Magazine. vol. 10, no. 7, August 1924. St. Louis Art League, 1924.

Art World. New York: Kalon Publishing Company, Inc., 1917.

Behrmann, Rev. Elmer H. *The Story of The Old Cathedral: Basilica of Saint Louis, King*. Church of St. Louis IX, King of France, 1949.

Brawer, Catherine Coleman and Kathleen Murphy Skolnik. *The Art Deco Murals of Hildreth Meière*. Anrea Monfried Editions, 2014.

Bullen, J. B. *Byzantium Rediscovered*. Phaidon, 2003.

Cathedral Basilica of Saint Louis. Website. cathedralstl.org.

Cathedral of Saint Louis: Structural Reinforced-Concrete in the New Cathedral. Brussel & Viterbo, consulting engineers for the Reinforced-Concrete Company, 1911.

Church Property Administration. vol. 2, Nov 1937. Milwaukee: Administrative Pub. Co., 1937.

Douglass, H. Paul. *The St. Louis Church Survey: A Religious Investigation with a Social Background*. George H. Doran Company, 1924.

Dupré, Judith. *Churches*. Harpers Collins Publishers, 2001.

Faherty, William Barnaby, SJ. *The Great Saint Louis Cathedral*. Archdiocese of Saint Louis, 1988.

Faherty, William Barnaby, SJ. *The St. Louis German Catholics*. Reedy Press, 2004.

The Inland Architect and News Record. vol. 47, no. 2, Mar 1906. Inland Publishing Co.

International Hildreth Meière Association Inc. Stamford, CT. hildrethmeiere.org.

McNamee, Maurice B., SJ. *Mosaics of the Cathedral Basilica of Saint Louis*. Cathedral Basilica of Saint Louis, 1994.

Missouri Life Magazine. Nov–Dec 1974. Jefferson City, MO: Missouri Life, Inc., 1974.

Rothensteiner, Rev. John. *History of the Archdiocese of St. Louis*. 2 vols. Blackwell Wielandy Co., 1928.

Rahill, Peter J. *Catholic Beginnings in Saint Louis*. Archdiocese of Saint Louis Bureau of Information, 1964.

Rozier, Firmin A. *History of the Early Settlement of the Mississippi Valley*. G. A. Pierrot & Son, Printers, 1890.

Schulte, Paul C. *The Catholic Heritage of Saint Louis: A History of the Old Cathedral Parish*. The Catholic Herald, 1934.

Scott, James F., writer and director. *Grandeur in Granite—the Saint Louis Cathedral*. Videotape. Optical Illusions, Inc. for the Archdiocese of St. Louis : BMC Teleproductions, 1986.

Souvay, Rev. Charles, CM. *The Historical Sketch: An Historical Sketch*. 1926.

Stiritz, Mary M. *St. Louis: Historic Churches & Synagogues*. St. Louis Public Library and Landmarks Association of St. Louis, Inc., 1995.

The St. Louis Cathedral: A Photographic Sketch. St. Louis Cathedral, 1948.

The St. Louis Cathedral: A Sketch. Cathedral of Saint Louis, 1928.

St. Louis Globe-Democrat. Newspaper.

St. Louis Post-Dispatch. Newspaper.

St. Louis Review. Newspaper. Archdiocese of Saint Louis.

Thornton, Francis A. *The Notable Catholic Institutions of St. Louis and Vicinity*. The Finkenbiner-Reid Publishing Co., 1911.

Toft, Carolyn Hewes. *St. Louis: Landmarks & Historic Districts*. Landmarks Association of St. Louis, Inc., 1988.

Walsh, John G., editor. *The Cathedral of Saint Louis*. Nies/Kaiser Printing Co., 1964.

Index